More Praise for *Leapfrogging*

"Soren Kaplan's book is a powerful and practical read on an aspect of break-through thinking that many of us have been missing—even though it's always been there right in front of us. Through the use of compelling stories, he brings to the foreground principles and practices that cause the reader to see the world of opportunities with a new lens. His integration of what it takes to innovate, both organizationally and personally, is exceedingly pragmatic. And his use of questions to help readers reveal their own insights and wisdom makes this a must-read for all those wanting to take their success to the next level."
—**Teresa Roche, Vice President and Chief Learning Officer, Agilent Technologies**

"Throughout my career I have relied on building prototypes to blaze the path to great solutions. Whether it is a new product, service, experience, or business, the goal is to challenge assumptions and find unexpected and hopefully breakthrough insights, and these often come in the form of small and large surprises. Soren Kaplan's treatise hits the nail on the head."
—**Dean Hovey, President and CEO, Digifit, and cofounder, IDEO**

"Change (and therefore innovation) is often seen as disruptive and uncomfort-able. *Leapfrogging* provides individuals and organizations a tried-and-true path for stepping into the unknown. With experience and compassion, Soren Kaplan leads the reader through a process that is not only imaginable but invaluable. While breakthroughs often require a certain degree of breakdown first, by follow-ing the *Leapfrogging* process you can feel confident the breakthrough will happen and the journey will be worth the risk!"
—**Renee Dineen, Head of Organizational Development, Roche Pharma Division**

"There is no doubt that one's mindset is a critical lever in driving true business in-novation. In *Leapfrogging*, Soren Kaplan has outlined exactly the right principles for creating an organizational mindset that challenges orthodoxies and seeks out and learns from surprises."
—**Deborah Arcoleo, Director, Global Innovation Center of Excellence, The Hershey Company**

"*Leapfrogging* is as much about the secrets of breakthrough leadership as it is about business innovation. The book is loaded with fresh ideas and examples that inspire new thinking and action."
—**Hans Middag, Director, Learning and Development, Randstad**

Leapfrogging

Harness the Power of Surprise for Business Breakthroughs

Leapfrogging

Harness the Power of Surprise
for Business Breakthroughs

Soren Kaplan

Berrett–Koehler Publishers, Inc.
San Francisco
a BK Business book

Berrett-Koehler Publishers, Inc.

235 Montgomery Street, Suite 650

San Francisco, CA 94104-2916

Tel: (415) 288-0260   Fax: (415) 362-2512   www.bkconnection.com

Ordering Information

Quantity sales. Special discounts are available on quantity purchases by corporations, associations, and others. For details, contact the "Special Sales Department" at the Berrett-Koehler address above.

Individual sales. Berrett-Koehler publications are available through most bookstores. They can also be ordered directly from Berrett-Koehler: Tel: (800) 929-2929; Fax: (802) 864-7626; www.bkconnection.com

Orders for college textbook/course adoption use. Please contact Berrett-Koehler: Tel: (800) 929-2929; Fax: (802) 864-7626.

Orders by U.S. trade bookstores and wholesalers.
Please contact Ingram Publisher Services, Tel: (800) 509-4887; Fax: (800) 838-1149; E-mail: customer.service@ingrampublisherservices.com; or visit www.ingrampublisherservices.com/Ordering for details about electronic ordering.

Berrett-Koehler and the BK logo are registered trademarks of Berrett-Koehler Publishers, Inc.

Printed in the United States of America

Berrett-Koehler books are printed on long-lasting acid-free paper. When it is available, we choose paper that has been manufactured by environmentally responsible processes. These may include using trees grown in sustainable forests, incorporating recycled paper, minimizing chlorine in bleaching, or recycling the energy produced at the paper mill.

Library of Congress Cataloging-in-Publication Data

Kaplan, Soren.
  Leapfrogging : harness the power of surprise for business breakthroughs / Soren
    Kaplan. -- 1st ed.
      p. cm.
  Includes bibliographical references and index.
  ISBN 978-1-60994-494-0 (hbk.)
  1. Creative ability in business. 2. Creative thinking. 3. New products. 4. Diffusion
  of innovations. 5. Problem solving. 6. Management. I. Title.
  HD53.K366 2012
  658.4'012--dc23

                                                                    2012014859

First Edition

17 16 15 14 13 12   10 9 8 7 6 5 4 3 2 1

Interior design and production by Dovetail Publishing Services.
Cover design by Irene Morris Design

To Holli, Raelyn, and Nola—

Thank you for joining me in creating
a life filled with positive surprise.

Contents

Foreword

by Marshall Goldsmith

Soren Kaplan is one of those interesting individuals who has spent decades working with a variety of different types of organizations and individuals. And, those of us fortunate enough to have selected his book to read will benefit by leaps and bounds from his knowledge and expertise.

Drawing on his extensive experience with all types of organizations, from corporations to non-profits to start-ups, Soren has boiled the basic mission of business down to a simple sentence: "individuals, groups, and organizations across all sectors of society want bigger ideas so they can have a greater positive impact." The rest of *Leapfrogging* explains how leaders can guide their organizations to successful and continued completion of this critical mission.

One of the most poignant messages I found in the book is in Chapter 3. In this chapter, Soren makes the strong point that "leapfrogging to breakthroughs is a *process,* not a one-time event." Many of us want, even expect, things to happen right now, just because we believe they should. For instance, by picking up this book, you might expect that your organization will change tomorrow. It won't, but you have taken a big step in the right direction!

As we all know, things have changed quite a bit in the last few decades. Globalization, which we in the West thought would mean a world of people competing to buy our products, has actually come to mean millions of smart, hard-working people around the globe working and competing for food, oil, cement, wood, and natural resources. In this era of uncertainty, nothing can be taken for granted. We have to keep upgrading, changing, and growing if we're going to be successful.

This is exactly what Soren teaches us. Using stories and examples from his own experience with leaders in different organizations, Soren reveals how these leaders have led their organizations to breakthrough success. These are real-life examples, from successful leaders who understand the concepts behind *Leapfrogging*. You will learn much from these leaders, for instance: How did they challenge the norms, break the molds, and inspire followers? How did they approach tough times? How did they make the most of mini-successes? How did they stay focused on the larger goal—to create something new or significantly different that would push the organization forward?

Read this book. Take its message to heart and implement it in your business. You will be glad you did!

Life is good.
Marshall Goldsmith

Marshall Goldsmith was recently recognized as the world's most-influential leadership thinker in the bi-annual *Thinkers50* study—sponsored by the *Harvard Business Review.* His 31 books include the *New York Times* bestsellers, *MOJO* and *What Got You Hee Won't Get You There.*

Introduction

After twenty years working with corporations, start-ups, nonprofits, and health-care organizations, I've seen that individuals, groups, and organizations across all sectors of society want bigger ideas so they can have a greater positive impact. Whether developing a new product or service, creating a new HR program, improving finance procedures, introducing a new fundraising campaign, embarking on a membership drive, or launching a new business, people want success through *being different and making a difference.*

Today's business, political, economic, and social challenges are so daunting that we're experiencing a palpable, collective yearning for breakthroughs—recognition that small changes no longer move the needle and that incremental thinking won't suffice. We want meaningful results, but we know we can achieve them only by challenging norms, inspiring others, and crafting a future unconstrained by the present.

Leapfrogging is about changing the game—*creating something new or doing something radically different that produces a significant leap forward.* What you create or change can vary, but one thing remains constant: Individuals, groups, and organizations that leapfrog old ways of doing things often become the new leaders of the future.

I'll be honest. When I began this book, I thought I knew where big breakthroughs came from. It took a small café in Paris to teach me what leapfrogging is really all about.

One of the best things about being a business consultant and part-time professor is that I can work from anywhere. When I'm not on airplanes or leading workshops, I can work from home, at the local coffee shop, or just about anywhere else for that matter. So, at the end of 2010, I took advantage of my professional portability and moved my family to France for a year. My wife was thrilled to go. My two daughters weren't quite so enthusiastic. But they were only in elementary school at the time, so they weren't old enough to put up much of a fight.

Our goal was to get outside of our comfort zones and expand our minds. I also knew that I wanted to write a book about the subject that's been my work and passion for more than two decades—how leaders and organizations create business breakthroughs. I couldn't think of a better place to step back from the flurry of my regular life than in Paris. We took an apartment in the Marais and enrolled our girls in public school. They didn't speak a word of French when they started, but after several months, they could sling insults and use slang words like the rest of their French friends. We visited tourist attractions and mixed with the locals. We tried French delicacies like *foie gras* (goose liver), *rognons* (veal kidneys), and *andouillette* (pig colon)—although my wife and kids watched me eat the colon solo, saying it would push their taste buds just a little too far beyond their American roots. My taste buds will never be the same.

One day shortly after we arrived in Paris, I wandered into a little café called Caféotheque, hoping to find an Internet connection, a caffeine boost, and a corner table with an electrical outlet where I could hole up with my laptop and get busy writing. Little did I know that inside this modest coffee house I was about to experience something that would shape the entire focus of this book.

I ordered a *cafe crème* (like a strong latte) from a woman who turned out to be the owner, a native of Guatemala named Gloria Montenegro de Chirouze. I took a seat, preoccupied with the task of writing I had ahead of me. The moment I took a sip of my coffee, I forgot about everything else that had been on my mind. What a sublime cup of java it was! So smooth and yet so potent. I was absolutely stunned.

As I savored my beverage, I glanced up at a couple of newspaper clippings tacked onto the wall above me. One was written by David Lebovitz, the author of *The Sweet Life in Paris*,[1] whose book and blog are the bible for foreigners in France. Out of 35,000 bistros and cafes, Lebovitz called Caféotheque "the best coffee spot in Paris." The other article was from *The New York Times*. In a city chock-full of world-class destinations like the Louvre, the Eiffel Tower, Notre Dame, and the Bastille, the paper had recommended this tiny café, with just eight small tables and a few well-worn lounge chairs, as a must visit attraction.

I immediately realized I needed to get a better understanding of what exactly made this place so special. I struck up a conversation with Gloria. She told me that when she first came to France, she was shocked at how *bad* the coffee was there. Even in the best restaurants, terrible coffee would follow an exquisite meal. So, she and her husband, Bernard, quit their jobs to introduce Parisians to the truly great stuff she had known in Guatemala. This all made sense to me. But when she started describing how they do it, and what's behind it all, that's when she really blew me away.

Caféotheque breaks all of the rules for a café in Paris. There are no quintessential outside tables. They don't serve food. And you won't find any snooty waiters in white aprons. A miniature in-house roaster by the front door beckons every passerby with a welcoming aroma of pure smoky bliss. While 99 percent of other French cafés serve blended coffees of varying quality to reduce cost, Caféotheque offers only single-origin espresso drinks using beans from individual plantations. And customers can book personal coffee tastings (similar to wine tastings) that allow them to experience Caféotheque's twenty varieties of beans from around the world. Gloria personally goes and buys beans directly from each of these plantations, ensuring that they receive a fair trade price for their precious commodities, which in turn gives Caféotheque an assured supply of the best-quality product available. Gloria even sends her best full-time baristas to visit these plantations so they can see and experience every step of what makes great coffee truly great.

Caféotheque is all about "purity of purpose"—and that purpose is to give the highest quality coffee-drinking experience to others. In keeping with this, Gloria doesn't horde her beans. She sells her special roasts to other cafés and restaurants around the city. But perhaps the business's most unique venture is Caféotheque University, where budding baristas can receive a degree in "cafeology," which includes a month-long hands-on "menteeship" working under Gloria and Bernard. Most of their students have gone on to open their own cafés around France and even in far-off locations such as Ethiopia and China—and many return as customers to buy their bulk beans from Caféotheque.

As Gloria recounted her story for me, I had a startling realization. Here I was trying to use a little caffeine to jump-start my writing about what exactly constitutes a business breakthrough. And just by chance, I had wandered into the midst of the very thing I was laboring to describe. I was literally sitting inside of a business breakthrough, something that had vastly exceeded its peers by "leap-frogging" the conventions of what it means to be a French café (or any type of café for that matter).

Put simply, Caféotheque surprised me. It delivered exactly what groundbreaking innovations always deliver: something new, something powerfully effective, and—most important—something *unexpected*. And that rather straightforward concept led almost immediately to another. But this second insight was a lot harder for me to quantify and articulate, which is why it took me an entire book to do so.

Here's a preview. Surprise is not just something that differentiates breakthrough products and services. The unexpected is also a key ingredient in *creating* those delightfully surprising breakthroughs. In fact, as I'll show, the single most important factor in fostering true game changers isn't the classic lightbulb-above-the-head big idea. It's the way leaders and organizations handle the discomfort, the disorientation, and the thrill (and pain) of living with uncertainty, finding clarity from ambiguity, and being surprised.

Before that morning at Caféotheque, I had witnessed this dynamic time and time again as an executive, a consultant, and an academic. But it took a little café in Paris to crystallize just how critical the concept really is. That's right—I had to be surprised by surprise itself. The power of surprise, it turns out, is as robust as the coffee at Caféotheque.

Surprises Are the Most Predictable Thing in Business

My experience at Caféotheque provided me with a new lens through which to view my previous twenty years of working in the fields of strategy, innovation, and organizational change. As I said, my first insight was quite simple—that most business breakthroughs surprise us when we first experience them. From there, the concept of surprise as an important driver of breakthroughs became firmly implanted in my mind. I reflected on my career, researched the underlying dynamics of breakthroughs, and spoke with some seriously successful people across many different types of organizations using my new lens. Time and again, unexpected events and sometimes even big surprises surfaced as playing essential roles in how ideas initially arose and *especially* throughout the process of making them real.

At first, I wasn't completely ready to acknowledge this notion. I was hesitant, even resistant to writing about it. Could it really be true that unanticipated events and surprising experiences *themselves* were key factors in the larger process of achieving breakthrough business success? What's more, how could I create a model or map out a formula for something so, well, *unpredictable*?

The more I explored the topic, the more I saw surprise cropping up in various places during the process of creating breakthroughs—and the more important, even critical, it seemed. Here's a brief example of the type of thing I kept finding that shows the relationship between being surprised and creating the type of breakthrough that delivers "surprise" to the market.

Scott Cook, the founder of Intuit, once said, "I'm a big believer—and this is something I've come to learn—in savoring surprises. If there's something that's really a big surprise, upside or downside, that's generally the real world speaking to you, saying there's something you don't yet understand."[2] Cook credits the power of surprise for providing the impetus for a whole host of Intuit's successes.

Intuit's flagship product was Quicken, which rapidly became the leading software program for managing home finances. But one thing really bugged Cook and his leadership team. They kept hearing that small businesses were using the product—incorrectly. Quicken was meant for balancing basic checkbooks, not for the type of "real accounting" that's needed to run a business. After more than a year of dismissing what he believed was a strange anomaly, Cook decided he needed to figure out what was really going on. A little exploration provided a big surprise to Intuit's financially minded computer geeks—that the vast majority of small business owners don't care about, don't want, and don't know how to do debit accounting, which was precisely why they were using something as basic as Quicken. This insight revealed an even bigger and more practical surprise—that the market for small business accounting software was ripe for the taking. Within three months of launching its first business-specific application, QuickBooks, Intuit captured almost 70 percent market share. And the product remains one of the biggest and most profitable businesses for the company today.[3] Intuit's value for "savoring surprise" gives the company a unique edge that most organizations don't have. Employees across the company don't fight against unexpected events and experiences—either by avoiding them or by dismissing them when they happen. They use them proactively as practical tools for strategic innovation.

Current Mindsets Constrain Future Breakthroughs

Few leaders or companies capitalize on the unexpected like Scott Cook and Intuit. There's a reason for this. Take a look on Amazon and you'll find that most business books unanimously consider uncertainty, surprise, and basically anything else that's unpredictable to be big problems. In fact, Amazon currently lists fewer than a dozen management books with the word *surprise* in their titles, and *all* of them are focused on how to avoid, minimize, prevent, or re-duce the likelihood of experiencing the dreaded phenomenon.

When I ran the corporate innovation group at Hewlett-Packard (HP) during the roaring 1990s in Silicon Valley, my entire life revolved around big ideas. Everything I did focused on defining compelling visions, formulating goals, and creating concrete plans to help the company get from A to B. Uncertainty was the enemy, and we did everything we could to avoid it. Following my stint wading through the bureaucracy of a global enterprise, I went in the other direction and founded and ran a start-up. I jumped into that new world at the height of the dot-com era and left it shortly after the low. But even in that freewheeling environment, I still did everything I could to minimize uncertainty.

Whether we're in a large corporation or a start-up, just about everything we're told about the right way to lead our organizations involves increasing predictability and maximizing control—from planning, forecasting, and managing human resources, to train-ing and even managing innovation. Certainty is good. Uncertainty, ambiguity, and surprises are bad. We're told that business success comes from analyzing opportunities, carefully crafting strategies, and executing flawless action plans to achieve well-defined goals. But there's a problem with this pervasive mindset. In our quest for con-trol, we've demonized some of the most natural aspects of life and essential elements that are an inherent part of the process of achiev-ing breakthrough business success.

When it comes to the implications of all this for business, I think Gary Hamel said it best: "New problems demand new prin-ciples. Put bluntly, there's simply no way to build tomorrow's essen-tial organizational capabilities—resilience, innovation and employee engagement—atop the scaffolding of 20th century management principles." In the same book[4] he says, "In an age of wrenching change and hyper-competition, the most valuable human capabilities are precisely those that are least manageable." These two brief quotations propose something revolutionary: that we must embrace counterintuitive ideas that go against the grain of management and leadership as we know it if we are going to succeed in today's whirlwind world.

Our control-at-all-costs attitude may indeed be softening. In their book *Great by Choice*, Jim Collins and Morten Hansen found that how leaders respond to "luck events" plays a big role in their business success.[5] The best leaders, they say, capitalize on good luck when it happens and are the most prepared when they experience bad luck. These same leaders credit their luck *in retrospect* as a significant contributor to their longer-term achievements. Our mindsets seem to be evolving as we look for the deeper secrets of business success. Events beyond our control—yes, even good and bad luck!—are slowly being recognized as key elements of the formula.

It's one thing to recognize *retrospectively* that unplanned events affect our lives and our business decisions. It's another thing altogether to develop the awareness and the tools to deal with our surprises proactively in *real time*. That's what I hope this book can help you accomplish, so that you can turn whatever is thrown at you (good or bad) into something productive for yourself, your team, and your organization.

It's Ultimately about Leapfrogging

One of the goals of this book is to uncover and share the deeper leadership experiences and dynamics that are success factors during the often "messy" process of creating business breakthroughs. I define *leapfrogging* as *the process of overcoming limiting mindsets and barriers to create business breakthroughs.* I named this book *Leapfrogging* because when it comes down to it, that's exactly what achieving business breakthroughs is all about. It's about leapfrogging our mindsets so we can overcome the hidden assumptions and barriers that constrain us. It's about leapfrogging the expectations of customers, partners, employees, and the rest of the world so we can surprise them with a dramatic increase in value over what they're getting today. It's about leapfrogging the competition so that we can create a remarkable difference between ourselves and what others are doing. This transformation in value—whether through a product, service, business model, or process—is what I refer to as a *business breakthrough* throughout the book. Admittedly, the word *business* is a relative term. As I'll show through a variety of examples beginning in the first chapter, these types of breakthroughs are equally applicable to nonbusiness organizations.

My messages are simple:

Business breakthroughs deliver surprise. Our brains are wired to appreciate positive surprise. Great ideas surprise us with a strong dose of remarkable newness in ways that add value to our lives and challenge our assumptions about what we thought possible.

Surprises are strategic tools that drive breakthroughs. By proactively seeking out and using surprises as "guideposts" when they occur, we can gain new insights, generate ideas, and discover new directions for ourselves and our organizations.

Business breakthroughs transform people and organizations. Breakthrough business success doesn't simply result from a great idea. It involves a challenging and transformative journey through deep ambiguity, unforeseen events, and inevitable failures in order to come out on the other side to achieve business breakthroughs.

Leapfrogging isn't easy. When we're in the process of challenging the status quo, people take notice. At first they can be critical, telling us that what we're doing is impossible, unimportant, or even wrong. But if we persist and start to succeed, eventually criticism can give way to recognition and praise. Leapfrogging is about the journey of traversing ambiguity to find clarity. It's about finding direction in ourselves as leaders, which in turn creates new opportunities for our organizations. It's about revealing new possibilities to customers, clients, business partners, or others so they see themselves in our own hopes and aspirations, and then jump on board to join us on our journeys.

This book is the result of hard research and soft insight. It draws upon my twenty years of hands-on experience, research studies from universities around the world, and case examples from diverse organizations including global companies, start-ups, and nonprofits. I spoke to many people while writing this book. Some were clients and colleagues. Others were referred to me because they had achieved an undeniable breakthrough, or were currently involved in the process of doing so. Some were running multi-billion-dollar businesses with tens of thousands of employees. Others were in much smaller organizations with only several people.

Most of the book's examples come directly from my work or discussions with these leaders who possess track records and stories of breakthrough success from organizations including Gatorade, OpenTable, Intuit, Four Seasons, Philips, Colgate-Palmolive,

Kimberly-Clark, and numerous others. And I don't focus only on organizations that have created breakthrough products. I intentionally include examples from outside of the traditional mold, since today's world is much more about services, business models, processes, brands, and global collaboration. A number of examples also demonstrate how breakthroughs can relate to specific business functions, like finance, information technology, and marketing.

Many leaders have confidentially admitted to me that they have questioned themselves, their strategies, and the abilities of their teams and organizations during their journeys to their breakthroughs. On the exterior they portray themselves as confident, self-assured, and ready to take the world by storm. In the privacy of their corner offices, however, they acknowledge feelings of doubt, fear, and surprise, but they adamantly believe that they need to keep these experiences hidden away like skeletons in a closet. Massimo d'Amore, President of PepsiCo's Global Beverages Group, shed light on this dynamic when he said to me, "If anyone who's led a breakthrough says they didn't have a single doubt, you know they are lying. The challenge is to deal with ambiguity and doubt while balancing it with the determination leaders must show to their own teams. When we were reinventing Gatorade, I had many doubts during the difficult days but I always managed to keep them away from the team so they wouldn't be distracted from their journey. Deep-down I always knew it was the right journey to take, but when everyone's telling you what you're doing is crazy, it's hard not to have doubts." Discussions like this one reveal that some of the most important underlying leadership dynamics and secrets to breakthrough success are systematically hidden, since the very nature of creating business breakthroughs involves experiences that are pervasively considered to reveal weakness—including admitting to being surprised.

No Surprises Just Yet—Here's What's Next

This book is for all those who believe that the best way to leapfrog our mindsets and achieve breakthrough success is to push beyond our day-to-day thinking and begin living outside our comfort zones. It's for those who have a hunch that business—like life—is chock-full of serendipitous surprises that all hold hidden answers and opportunities.

But here's a warning before we get started. We're going to explore a side of business that usually flies under the radar. In fact, most leaders and organizations typically avoid the essential principles and practices that I describe. So, if you're willing to open yourself up in order to learn how to tackle your biggest challenges and capitalize on new opportunities in some pretty simple yet very unconventional ways, then welcome aboard.

1

Business Breakthroughs Deliver Surprise

I doubt whether the world holds for any one a more
soul-stirring surprise than the first adventure with ice cream.

—Heywood Broun

Chapter One Key Messages

1. We're wired to appreciate positive surprise.

2. Business breakthroughs deliver surprise.

3. Breakthroughs go far beyond products and services.

4. Breakthroughs aren't just for business.

This may sound a little over the top, but breakthroughs are a bit like pornography. Allow me to explain what I mean. The late Supreme Court Justice Potter Stewart was once asked to rule on what made something obscene. In his decision, he wrote a simple one-line answer, "I know it when I see it." Business breakthroughs often have this same unmistakable yet simultaneously indefinable quality. They're not always easy to predict or describe before they happen—but you recognize them when you see them.

Think about the first time you picked up an iPod, iPhone, or iPad and experienced the touch screen as an extension of your fingertips. Reflect back on the first time you played the Nintendo Wii, drove a Toyota Prius, used Purell hand sanitizer, discovered the trendy design of Method soap, visited Starbucks, or saw Cirque du Soleil. The list of the usual suspects of breakthroughs could go on and on. Though these things are all quite different from one another, they tend to produce similar feelings of positive surprise—with a hint of delight, wonder, and intrigue—when we first encounter them.

My first personal experience with what I felt was a real breakthrough came when I was seven years old and I poured a packet of Pop Rocks into my mouth. I'll never forget that tingling, crackling sensation all over my tongue. It was so new, so delightfully unexpected. Candy just wasn't supposed to *do* something like that! I also remember when I first signed up for Netflix and realized that I would never again have to schlep to the video store or pay a late fee (like the painful $18 penalty I once had to fork over to Blockbuster because my kids left *Chitty Chitty Bang Bang* under the couch). I had come to blindly accept the fact that a standard $3 movie rental really equated to about $10. What an incredible relief it was to be saved from my passive acceptance of the late-fee factor.

And that's what breakthroughs are all about. Seemingly out of nowhere, we experience a strong dose of remarkable newness that adds value—fun, happiness, time savings, financial savings, and so on—to our lives. Most people view business breakthroughs as stemming from new technologies or products. Sure, innovative products are often the most celebrated examples, but in today's world, more and more breakthroughs have less and less to do with high-tech wizardry. And breakthroughs can happen within specific business functions too, such as finance departments, HR organizations, sales forces, or anywhere else for that matter. Regardless of what a specific business breakthrough is or does, it usually challenges our assumptions and revises our sense of what we thought was possible. And, as a result, it *surprises.*

Perhaps my experiences don't match yours. Maybe you never tried Pop Rocks when you were a kid or, if you did, you didn't like them as much as I did. And perhaps you don't have a Netflix subscription. But my guess is that you can point to something at some point that gave you that feeling of freshness and wonder—and that something is our starting point. The surprising nature of breakthroughs transcends industries and different-sized organizations. And I've included some pretty diverse examples in this chapter to make this point.

Business Breakthroughs Can Come from Anywhere

In 1987, Niall Fitzgerald became Director of Foods & Detergents at Unilever. One of Niall's philosophies was that management and leadership were two different animals. "Good management brings a degree of order and consistency. But the leader must allow some chaos—even create chaos to liberate the risk taker,"[6] he once said. And liberate the risk taker he did. The same year that he took the head job, he sponsored a new team to do something radically different in the world of food at the time: sell ice cream to adults.

Back then, ice cream was kids' stuff. Aside from enjoying a sundae or a cone now and then with their children, most adult consumers barely gave the frozen treat a second thought. Unilever had been trying to figure out a way to change these ideas and break into the grownup market for more than a decade. But it wasn't until Fitzgerald showed up and got a little risky—or should I say, risqué—that things took a turn for the better.

Set upon an artfully designed stick, Unilever's Magnum ice cream bars touted high-end, sensual indulgence—rich cream, thick chocolate, and premium packaging. Its titillating advertisements reinforced this racy image. (Many of them would probably be banned from running in the United States; check out the "Magnum Five Senses" video on YouTube to see what I mean.) On first blush, it would have been easy to think Magnum's excess would have gone the way of Krispy Kreme's boom-to-bust doughnuts. But under Niall's leadership, the brand grew and expanded across Europe, and it has recently been introduced into the United States. Even without a significant presence in the enormous American market, Magnum sells enough bars in a year to treat about one-seventh of the world's population to its creamy indulgence—yes, that's a *billion* ice cream bars per year.

Magnum's incredible success is tied to several surprising things. First, linking ice cream to adult themes was nothing short of scandalous in the late 1980s. One of Magnum's first ad campaigns invited consumers to have a "Magnum affair." This brash, unapologetically adult-oriented strategy paid immediate dividends. People were naturally tempted to take Magnum up on its offer. Second, while most ice cream companies tend to focus on reducing costs and expanding distribution, Magnum went in the opposite direction. Instead of cutting prices and going after new markets, the company put out limited-edition flavors like its "Seven Sins" and "Five Senses" bars. In so doing, it managed to do what would have seemed impossible several decades earlier. It made ice cream on a stick a luxury item. Indeed, Magnum's entire brand image and everything it does encourage us to give in to the impulse to treat ourselves to "indulgent pleasure"—something any of us who have paid five bucks for a Starbucks latte can relate to. Today, offering adults a temporary escape through fine chocolate, a cup of gourmet coffee, and, of course, ice cream is a fairly common occurrence. Back when Niall first launched Magnum, though, it was a surprising concept that challenged assumptions.

Unilever's Magnum is a great example of how to shift mindsets through new products and marketing. But business breakthroughs today aren't limited to these things. Many leaders in large corporations tell me that they want big breakthroughs, but then they assign the task to their R&D and product development groups. People in HR, Legal, Accounting, Supply Chain, Sales, and other functions often feel left out of the equation. The good news is that business breakthroughs are agnostic. Here's an example from the corner of a company that most of us might think would be the last place we'd find a breakthrough—in DuPont's legal department.

It's probably *not* surprising that a team of lawyers could benefit from a breakthrough, but what this group achieved would be the envy of any business function. With 60,000 employees in ninety different countries, not to mention a huge variety of products in everything from agriculture to electronics to clothing, the volume of legal work needed to keep DuPont's operation going is utterly staggering. Patent law, tax law, employment law, contracts, antitrust, intellectual property, class action defense—a company like DuPont simply cannot survive without lawyers, lots and lots of lawyers.

By the early 1990s, the company's then-Associate General Counsel, Thomas Sager, knew that things had gotten out of hand. At that time, more than 350 law firms were working on DuPont's dime. The sheer number of lawyers and their lack of coordination weren't the only problems Sager identified. There was also a troubling disconnect between the company's interests and the interests of its legal advocates. For the law firms, everything was about billable hours. That meant, no matter what, the firms wanted to fight cases to the bitter end. If one of DuPont's products or the way the company was doing business were truly causing harm, Sager reasoned it would be more profitable to change that product or that business practice rather than litigate the matter for years and years. But the law firms working for DuPont would never recommend such a thing because it would mean less revenue for them.

Sager knew that he had a mammoth project on his hands. He also knew that he wanted to do more than just cut costs—he could run his function like most other corporate legal departments, or he could create a new model that would push him outside of his comfort zone, a model that would ensure that his department became a core contributor to the strategic operations of the business and even influence the operating models of the dozens of firms working for DuPont. If he was truly going to help the company, nibbling around the edges of the challenges facing his legal department wasn't going to be enough. This was going to have to be a big time, paradigm-warping effort.

The first thing Sager did was slash the number of law firms working for DuPont. By the mid-1990s, DuPont was using fewer than fifty law firms and that number is now down to thirty-seven.[7] But culling firms wasn't Sager's only goal. He wanted the ones that remained to be strategic partners, not independent rivals. DuPont Legal's "Knowledge Management Program" now encourages the firms to share information and practices with one another. "We created a mix of large, small, and medium firms so as to deal with the complexity of cases," Sager said. "We then trained them to work together."[8]

But here was Sager's most surprising accomplishment. He challenged a fundamental assumption of the profession by asking a simple yet revolutionary question: What if instead of paying fees by the hour—which encourages long, drawn-out cases—firms were paid more to solve problems faster? The traditional billable hours system was simply not workable, so Sager tore it down and built up an entirely new model. A system of incentives now encourages attorneys to find the best ways to resolve issues as cheaply and effectively as possible. This "Early Case Assessment" approach allows DuPont's lawyers to put their efforts into cases they believe are winnable. Early Case Assessment also benefits the company as a whole. Legal troubles can be symptoms of actual problems in the way a business is operating. If you keep getting sued, maybe there's something wrong with you, not the people suing. Sager's new model lets DuPont's lawyers identify these problems instead of fighting to minimize them or cover them up. "DuPont Legal works almost like business," Sager said. "We bring value to the company."[9]

Sager's reinvention of the legal department has saved the company millions of dollars. It has also done something perhaps equally valuable: It has remade the entire legal culture at DuPont and its partner firms. Innovation, flexibility, and long-term mutual success are now the main objectives. And this new focus is reflected not only in how the company conducts its business but also in whom it hires to do it. Corporate law has a long reputation for being an old boys' club or, more accurately, an old white boys' club. Sager and the DuPont Legal team set out to change this. When selecting which law firms to retain as partners, they made diversity a priority. DuPont Legal currently sponsors mentoring, scholarship, and job fair programs to bring in more women and minority associates. This push for a more diverse workforce isn't just a feel-good operation or a way to burnish DuPont's corporate image. It's a strategic move, another way to foster innovation by rewarding fresh ideas and new approaches. As Sager said during a recent interview, "DuPont has been in existence for [over 200] years and now faces a new era of intense global competition. The business need for diversity—diversity of background, perspective and experience—is critical if we are to be successful and thrive for another 200 years."[10]

Questions to Consider

- ➲ What is an example of a breakthrough within your own industry?
- ➲ What old assumptions or barriers did this breakthrough challenge or overcome?
- ➲ What impact did it have?

Breakthroughs Aren't Just for Business

Although Unilever and DuPont are examples from the business world, breakthroughs are just as relevant and important to social, educational, health-care, political, and other organizations. Take, for example, the world of education. When it comes to public education in America, ideas are never in short supply. Scholars, activists, and politicians are constantly churning out opinions on how to fix our schools—smaller class size, more instructional aides, English-only instruction, bilingual instruction, more standardized tests, fewer standardized tests, magnet schools, mentors, merit-based teacher pay. The list of initiatives is endless. And yet, year after year, across the country, the results couldn't be more clear: Our schools continue to fail. Recent studies have shown that even most charter schools, the latest fad in education, are not faring much better on average than their government-run counterparts.[11]

Thank goodness people like Dave Levin and Mike Feinberg, founders of the *Knowledge Is Power Program* (KIPP) Academies, haven't been discouraged given this seemingly futile context. As former teachers with the Teach for America program, they completed their service and then immediately embraced a blindingly obvious opportunity to which they've now dedicated their lives: *to create a school that truly works*. Well, they did that, and more. Today, KIPP represents a network of almost 100 public charter schools serving more than 27,000 students that have collectively challenged the conventions of public education in the United States: ten-hour days, school on Saturdays, teachers who eagerly give their home phone numbers to students, and a contract outlining shared goals and commitments that must be signed by students and their parents before admittance. If this type of approach for a public school isn't surprising, I'm not sure what would be.

The foundation of KIPP rests on Levin and Feinberg's pointed rejection of the idea that some ingenious new program from an administrator or lawmaker will magically transform the system. They paint a simple slogan in the hallways of their schools to show this: "There are no shortcuts."

Put simply, Levin and Feinberg went old school—as in Thomas Edison old school. Indeed, Edison, who said, "Genius is one percent inspiration and ninety-nine percent perspiration," would appreciate the KIPP approach to learning. School starts at 7:30 AM and goes until 5:00 PM. Then comes the homework, usually about two hours per night. The labor doesn't end on the weekend or over the summer either. Kids attend school two Saturdays a month and three weeks into the traditional summer break as well.

All this time and effort grow out of one very basic philosophy: The business of educators is to educate and the business of students is to learn. This concept might seem head-slappingly self-evident, but it's not at all easy to live up to. It means that if students do not grasp a subject, their teacher must work with them until they do. If they have to stay for an extra hour after school or talk it through on the phone until ten o'clock at night, so be it.

Think about something else inherent in that philosophy: There are no excuses. Every child, given the proper time and instruction, can excel. That's an incredibly powerful, even revolutionary, idea. And Levin and Feinberg have proven that it works. Nearly every KIPP school in the county is in an inner-city neighborhood. They do not require an entrance exam. More than nine out of ten KIPP students are Hispanic or African American. Seven out of ten of them live below the poverty line. Most enter the program performing well below grade level. Typically, less than 10 percent of children with such backgrounds go on to finish college. KIPP students boast a 90 percent graduation rate—not from high school, from college![12]

So, now that we've seen a breakthrough in action in education, let's move to the nonprofit world. Think of the toughest, most intractable social problems in America. Homelessness is probably at or near the top of any list. HIV and AIDS are probably right up there too, as is substance abuse. Helping people who face any one of these challenges is an incredibly worthy cause for a nonprofit organization.

But how about taking on all three? How about an organization that serves homeless people suffering from HIV and drug addiction? Just imagine the amount of work and dedication that would take, not to mention money. Now try to imagine doing all of that and turning a "profit" too. I put the word *profit* in quotation marks because New York-based Housing Works, which manages to do everything I just described, is technically a charity operation. But it acts an awful lot like a business. And a very successful one, at that.

In an era when most nonprofits are cutting back, largely because they rely on private donors and government funding, Housing

Works is expanding. It just opened subsidiaries in Haiti; Washington, DC; and Mississippi.[13] Since Housing Works opened in 1990, an estimated 20,000 people have benefited from its work, and that number continues to grow, thanks to the company's pioneering "social enterprise" approach.

If Mother Teresa had earned an MBA, she might have become a lot like Housing Works' co-founder Charles King. King and his late partner Keith Cylar opened Housing Works' first thrift store in Manhattan in the mid-1990s. This was not your typical Salvation Army–style second-hand shop. King and Cylar's surprising approach began with the idea that thrift stores don't have to be dingy caves with bins of unwanted scrappy clothes. In fact, they did not accept all, or even most, donations. Only the highest-end goods were allowed in. "We see ourselves as the Barneys of thrift shops," King once said.[14]

That first location was so successful that Housing Works soon opened another shop to handle the demand, and then another, and another still. There are now ten Housing Works thrifts around the city. In 2009, the company expanded to Brooklyn. The new store across the East River made a million dollars in its first year—in the midst of the recession.[15]

By hosting upscale events like fashion shows and celebrity clothes auctions, King and the rest of the Housing Works team have turned the thrifts into must-visit attractions. *W* magazine once hailed the stores as the "hottest" in the city, "the place where the city's fashionistas drop off last year's Prada and Comme des Garçons."[16]

The company has built prestigious brands for its other moneymaking enterprises as well. It recently hired well-known chef Michael Sherman to design the menus for its café and catering businesses. Famous writers give readings at a bookstore run by Housing

Works. And big-time music acts like Bjork have performed at Housing Works benefits.

All told, Housing Works' social enterprise investments yield a quarter of its $43-million annual budget. Most of its other revenues come from fee-for-service contracts with the government. This arrangement, as opposed to the traditional cost-reimbursement model, also allows Housing Works to keep any proceeds from cost savings or efficiencies that it puts in place.[17]

King's commitment to making money has been controversial in the nonprofit world. Some see it as a conflict of interest or a potential distraction from the group's mission. But for King, it's a matter of survival, born of long experience. His belief is simple: "Nonprofits need [to stop] going up the hill with our hand out begging . . . we must stop thinking of 'funding' as charity and start thinking of 'financing' as an investment that has real, quantifiable economic or social return."[18]

From ice cream bars for adults to money-making non-profits, surprises are surprising because they're unanticipated. That may sound blindingly obvious, but it's an important point. If we know that something will happen, we're not as gratified because our expectations and assumptions are largely met. Business breakthroughs give us something we're not expecting to see or experience. And they almost always do this by overcoming seemingly set-in-stone assumptions about what's possible with products, services, business models, processes, or our organizations themselves.

We're Wired to Appreciate Positive Surprise

When I ask business leaders, students, or friends to think back on their favorite experiences with what they consider truly breakthrough new

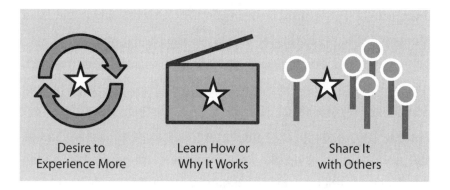

| Desire to Experience More | Learn How or Why It Works | Share It with Others |

The Personal Dynamics of Positive Surprise

products or services, many can't help but smile. The range of things I've heard when I've asked the question is immense: iPads, Disneyland, Diaper Genies, Facebook, snowboards, rollerblades, Zappos, the Swiffer, Etch A Sketch, Crest White Strips, the Amazon Kindle, Skype, the University of Phoenix, MTV, eBay, Segway scooters, Harry Potter books, and the list goes on.

There is a reason for their Cheshire Cat grins. They're reliving the pleasure of being surprised. Not the kind of surprise when our older brother jumps out from behind a door and scares the crap out of us. It's the opposite kind of surprise—the kind that signals delight, appreciation, and intrigue. When we experience a positive surprise, it compels us to do three things:

1. Want to experience more of it

2. Learn about how or why it works the way it does

3. Share it, so we can take a small amount of credit for others' own smiles of surprise

It turns out that there is a physiological basis for these types of positive responses. Our brains are built to like the "pleasingly unexpected." Two neuroscience researchers, Gregory Burns and Read Montague, discovered this fact in a pretty interesting way.[19, 20]

Burns and Montague convinced some unsuspecting research subjects to join them for a drink—in their lab. Their subjects were first hooked up to an MRI machine to measure their brain's "pleasure centers." This is the part of the brain that's responsible for pleasurable feelings. It lights up like a slot machine when people take addictive drugs or anticipate receiving money. After Burns and Montague connected their subjects to the MRI device, they asked them to open wide, just as they might do at the dentist—though what came next wasn't painful.

The participants hadn't been told what was going to happen, so no one knew that a computer was about to squirt water or juice into their mouths! Half of the people received water; the other half got juice. To further segment their research subjects, half of the people in each of the water and juice groups received their drinks at regular, predictable intervals while the others were continually surprised with random, sporadic squirts.

Burns and Montague presumed that people's brains would respond most positively to their preferred beverage. But they found that it didn't matter whether their subjects wanted water or juice. Across the board, the brain's pleasure centers were most activated in those who received unpredictable, random squirts, regardless of the beverage they were given.

These two researchers pinpointed the fundamental mechanism behind why we perceive breakthroughs as special: *We're wired to appreciate positive surprises.* Whether it's QuickBooks, iPads, or Cirque du Soleil, most of us recognize breakthroughs when we see or experience them because our brains are set up to appreciate the way they challenge assumptions while adding value to things we care about.

Questions to Consider

➲ What products, services, or experiences bring a smile to your face?

➲ When was the last time something really surprised you in a delightfully positive way?

➲ Why did these things surprise you?

Why Business Breakthroughs Surprise Us

The examples in this chapter demonstrate how business breakthroughs overcome existing mindsets by introducing whole new possibilities—and consequently new assumptions—into the mix. Breakthroughs share three common characteristics, which produce big changes that make a big difference—not just mere improvements to what's already being done today, which is exactly what makes them feel surprising when we experience them.

1. Breakthroughs challenge fundamental assumptions about existing products, services, business models, or organizations.

2. Breakthroughs transform existing ways of doing business by rewriting rules or revolutionizing current practices.

3. Breakthroughs apply resources in entirely new ways, whether people, knowledge, relationships, or technology.

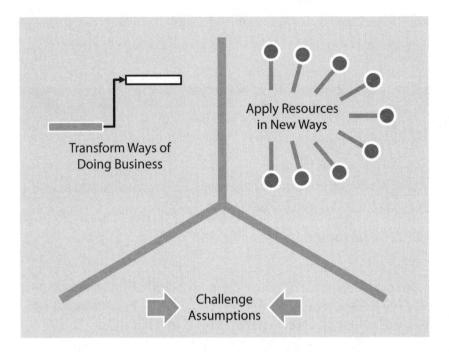

Three Characteristics of Breakthroughs

We hear about breakthroughs all the time, and the big ones are touted again and again: The Nintendo Wii challenged the convention of what it means to "play" video games; Cirque du Soleil reinvented "the circus"; and Apple revolutionized the "mp3 player," transformed the "smartphone," and established the mass market for "tablet computers" with its iPad. The mythology that grows up around these grandiose examples can lead us to dismiss the possibility that we hold the potential to lead breakthroughs ourselves. This is because many of us, implicitly or explicitly, view breakthroughs as larger than life and beyond our reach. But from Niall Fitzgerald's provocative ice cream, Thomas Sager's revolutionary legal department, Levin and Feinberg's forward-thinking yet back-to-basics KIPP Academies, and Charles King's moneymaking non-profit, we've seen that breakthroughs can come in many forms and from many places.

2

The Power of Surprise

If you choose to go looking for something, you'd better
be ready for whatever it is you find.
Because it may not be what you were expecting.

—Jodi Picoult

Chapter Two Key Messages

1. Surprises are guideposts to new directions and opportunities.

2. Big surprises can come in small doses.

3. We need to surprise ourselves before we can surprise others.

On a small cobblestone street in Breda, Holland, about seventy miles south of Amsterdam, sits a nondescript drugstore. No formal name can be seen from the street, other than a sign that reads "Drogist," Dutch for *pharmacist*. But the elderly owner, Joep, seemingly the only employee in the shop, is much more than that. Nearly eighty years old, Joep has transformed the customer experience in his quaint drugstore into something that would be the envy of CVS, Walgreens, and Rite-Aid.

Each year I spend two weeks in Breda—a big town for Holland with a population of almost 200,000—teaching at a small university.

A few years ago I arrived in Breda after a long trip involving planes, trains, and automobiles, and I realized that the shaving cream container in my toiletry bag was empty. Since I didn't want to show up for my first day of class with a five-o-clock shadow, I meandered through the twisting streets of Breda until I stumbled upon Joep. The appearance of his drugstore was nothing special, just a typical pharmacy with the usual sundries.

Joep asked what I wanted (fortunately for me, most people speak English in Holland, including Joep) and I let him know I was in the market for shaving cream. He took me over to the proper shelf and I selected a can from the three or four limited options. As I approached the counter to pay, Joep asked me with an inquisitive, childlike tone, "What year were you born?" Caught off guard and having no idea why he was asking, I instinctively responded, "1968."

During this brief exchange, Joep had pulled out what looked like an oversized wooden cigar box. I peered over the top, which he had raised with one hand while leafing through dozens of small cardboard dividers with the other. On each divider was a handwritten scribble in red ink indicating the number of a year. "Ahhh," he exclaimed, pulling out a plastic bag that had "1968" etched onto it. Opening up the bag, he took out a small coin, placed it on the back of his hand and held it six inches from my face. "For you!" he said happily, as he ensured that I was reading the date on the coin. I thanked him, paid, and departed with my shaving cream as well as the Dutch guilder minted with my birth year.

Although completely useless in the practical sense, Joep's personalized gift, combined with experiencing his own joyful pleasure, filled me with appreciation, not to mention intrigue. But as is typical for me, the skeptical, marketing side of my brain immediately kicked in. I couldn't help but wonder: Why did he do this? How did he think of it? Was it just some kind of nutty gimmick? And how did he keep up his supply of coins? The guilder had been taken out of circulation in 2002!

During several visits to Joep's drugstore over the next two years, I got the answers to all of these questions. I learned that he gives a piece of licorice to every child who walks through his door and a guilder to every adult. After the guilder was replaced by the Euro, Joep found a jar of them in his garage and decided that giving a coin to adults could be as personally pleasing as passing out licorice to children. When pressed on his motivation, Joep's answer is simple: He does it because it makes people happy, and in turn, this makes him happy. Joep is most proud of his ability to find and give these old coins to his eldest customers, citing a recent gift of a 1918 guilder. He always smiles as he describes the reactions of people, young and old, who enter his store expecting to find shaving cream, shampoo, or aspirin and end up finding far more.

Joep's small gesture on my first visit to his shop has certainly kept me coming back. I brought my wife on one trip, a colleague on another, and told every class about the experience. There are plenty of other drugstores in Breda. Some are even closer to the college than Joep's. And yet, I will gladly travel the small extra distance to his shop for one simple reason: One morning, years ago now, he surprised me in a pleasant way.

I didn't really realize the incredible impact of Joep's guilder giveaway until I heard about the effect it's had on his local customers. After Joep had given guilders to them for several years, an amazing thing happened. People started bringing him their own jars of coins from their garages and attics! These customers, who themselves had previously experienced the surprise of receiving his small gift, felt compelled to contribute to the cause. They themselves wanted to play a role in supporting and sustaining the surprising experience for others by co-creating Joep's retail experience with him. Talk about building customer loyalty. Joep has achieved what others might spend thousands, if not millions, to do—but he's done it all for the cost of a few obsolete coins.

My story about this "Drogist" illustrates a core theme of this chapter—that surprises come in all shapes and sizes. Sometimes they deliver an immediate, galvanizing flash of insight. But sometimes we experience a series of smaller, seemingly less consequential surprises over a period of time that collectively add up to something bigger. With respect to my own experience writing this book, I must admit that when I first witnessed Joep's guilder giveaway, I knew it was special, but I didn't see the deeper relationship to the whole idea of surprise. It wasn't until after my conversation with Gloria at Caféotheque that I realized that the power of surprise resides at the heart of Joep's business.

Surprises Are Guideposts

At Intuit, while the folklore of how QuickBooks came to be lives on, the appreciation for (and profiting from) surprise continues today. One of the latest examples involves an experiment by a couple of software engineers at the company. They had a fairly simple idea. They wanted to see whether they could take a picture of W-2 tax forms with their smartphones and use those images to automatically fill out the related fields within TurboTax. A lot of people had told them it would be impossible given the wide variety of sizes and formats of employers' W-2s. The first small surprise they encountered was when they realized that moving this data from paper form to digital photo to the computer-based software was actually doable.

From there, the software engineers brought the idea out to potential customers to see whether real people would even find an ounce of value in this new feature. That's when the big surprise occurred. People liked the efficiency of saving the time it takes to manually transfer their W-2 numbers to TurboTax. But many of them asked the engineers the same question: "Why can't I just finish my taxes on the phone?" This single question, heard over and over again, revealed that many people don't actually use the full feature set of TurboTax. They don't itemize their deductions or write off investment income. Just about all they use to fill out their taxes are their W-2 forms. And they wanted to know, quite reasonably, why they couldn't just take pictures of those forms, send them to the IRS, and be done with it?

With that market opportunity plainly in front of them, the TurboTax leadership team dedicated resources full force to create SnapTax, now one of the most popular finance apps for the iPhone and Android. SnapTax allows people to take a photo of their W-2 form, answer a few basic questions, and electronically file their taxes right from their phone—all in about ten minutes! No wonder feedback in Apple's app store includes comments like "Oh, my God" and "Easy and Magical," signaling the type of positive surprise customers experience when they see a business breakthrough.[21]

Harnessing the power of surprise is very different from the proverbial big idea that pops into our head in the shower. Using surprises as strategic tools involves paying close attention to the things that happen around us and directly to us. The goal is to use unexpected events or surprising experiences, along with our initial reactions to them, to reevaluate our goals, our strategies, our plans, and—most important—our assumptions about what's possible. Here's a great example of a surprising experience that catalyzed a game-changing, assumption-shattering innovation.

Maybe more than any other industry, the pharmaceutical business is all about innovation. With their dependence on exclusive and fast-expiring patents, drug companies must come up with the next blockbuster pill (and the one after that, and the one after that, . . .) or they die. To that end, "Big Pharma" shelled out a record $67.4 billion last year developing new treatments for a range of diseases—from cancer to restless leg syndrome.[22] But, even in a sector like this, where innovation is the name of the game, many assumptions and barriers limit the industry's potential. And most people either fail to recognize these barriers altogether or simply take them for granted as an inherent and unchangeable part of the system.

For instance, those billions in R&D investments don't necessarily produce the best (or the most needed) medicines. Taking a promising compound from the lab to the marketplace can cost a billion dollars or more. As a result, companies tend to develop drugs based on profit potential alone. That means most new medicines treat ailments that afflict consumers in affluent, developed markets. A case in point: The most profitable pharmaceutical product in the world is Lipitor, which helps lower cholesterol levels. Nexium, the second most profitable, alleviates heartburn.[23] Don't get me wrong. Keeping one's cholesterol in check is important. And heartburn can be very uncomfortable. But how's this for a little perspective: Two million children around the world die every year from diarrhea. That's right, diarrhea. More children die from it than from AIDS, tuberculosis, and malaria combined.[24] Speaking of malaria, an estimated 300 to 500 million people are afflicted with it every year. Nearly a million die. In total, only 10 percent of the money spent on new drugs goes to problems like these that affect the poorest 90 percent of the world's population.[25]

When Victoria Hale was an executive in the pharmaceutical industry in the 1990s, she used to worry about this inequity. Then she took a cab to the airport one day and had what she called a "moment of clarity." Her driver was of African descent. When she told him what she did for a living, he threw back his head and laughed. "You people have all the money," he said.

Hale took his surprising reaction immediately to heart. "Why was it in our world in the 21st century," she recalled thinking, "were there people who had medicine for any disease, any complaint, and in other parts of the world . . . babies die of dehydrating diarrhea? How can that be? That is not fair. If there was anything I could do personally, then I had to do it."[26]

Of course, Hale wasn't the first person to quit her high-paying job to help the world's less fortunate. But the way she went about it was truly remarkable. As a former insider, Hale knew that every major drug company maintains a vast "library" of potentially life-saving compounds deemed too risky or unprofitable to continue studying. She set out to make use of these untapped resources by starting the country's first nonprofit pharmaceutical company, the Institute for OneWorld Health. As a nonprofit, OneWorld is able to offer drug companies tax deductions for donating unused compounds, otherwise known as "leads." OneWorld then partners with universities and other research centers to refine the leads and uses donations from charitable foundations to pay for clinical trials. If the treatments are proven safe and effective, OneWorld hires local manufacturers to produce the new medicines.

OneWorld's first major project was curing visceral leishmaniasis, a deadly infection better known as Black Fever. A promising new treatment for Black Fever had already been developed, but clinical trials had been discontinued because of cost. OneWorld was able to revive the trials and contract with an Indian manufacturer to produce a vaccine. The medicine, an antibiotic known as paromomycin, will save the lives of an estimated 60,000 people a year.[27] OneWorld is also working on treatments for childhood diarrhea, malaria, and other insidious—but preventable—diseases.

Before Hale came up with her nonprofit method for developing drugs, ailments like Black Fever and diarrhea were seen as tragic but inevitable realities. Hale has shattered these defeatist assumptions—and her ingenious new approach has produced positive results for everyone involved. Not only do thousands of sick people get medicines they desperately need, but also drug companies get value for otherwise neglected compounds and researchers get to use their expertise to study and refine them. But that's not all. Under Hale's model, people from regions affected by these diseases do a large portion of OneWorld's work. They conduct clinical trials, and they produce and distribute the new medicines. In this way, the treatment of these illnesses has actually become an economic benefit instead of a drain. Now that's a win–win–win–win solution.

What Hale describes as a "moment of clarity" in a cab was essentially a surprise that catalyzed a whole new chapter in her life. And her nonprofit pharmaceutical model has been successful because it empowers others to discover surprising new possibilities by giving them an active role in a radically new approach to drug delivery and development.

Questions to Consider

- ➲ What surprises have you experienced in your personal or business life?

- ➲ What types of things did these surprises "tell" you?

- ➲ How did these unexpected events lead to new directions that you wouldn't have gone if they had not occurred?

Big Surprises Can Come in Small Doses

Not every surprise results in a lightning flash of clarity like Victoria Hale's. Sometimes they're much more subtle, like my experience in Joep's pharmacy. Surprises can also come in a series of smaller doses, which then require a bit more interpretation to uncover their bigger implications.

Here's another story that demonstrates the point, one that was told to me over dinner one night by Barbara Talbott, the former Executive Vice President of Marketing for Four Seasons Hotels. Barbara's story is about how she led herself, her team, and her organization on a journey that delivered surprises to everyone involved, while establishing Four Seasons as one of the most recognized luxury hotel and resort brands in the world. Barbara's story also epitomizes the feet-on-the-ground, action-oriented aspects of how surprises can crop up and be used during the tactical phases of creating breakthroughs.

Barbara's story begins in the early days of the Internet, the mid-1990s, when virtually all businesses were in a frenzy over this thing called "the web." Across industries, leaders fretted about how to engage this exciting but intimidating new technology. Everyone knew it was going to change the way the marketplace functioned in fundamental ways, but nobody had any clue exactly how.

The uncertainty of the net in the 1990s was especially tough on those in the luxury market. Dot-com prognosticators were heralding the end of human interactions. Everything would soon be done online, they said, making transactions cheaper and processes more efficient. Costs would go down, and so would prices—on everything. Of course, this was anathema to high-end businesses. From Ferragamo to Ferrari, luxury brands all feared that the web was shaping up to look like one big digital discount bin. And most of them reacted with a "wait and see" attitude—or by hoping the whole thing would simply go away.

"Luxury brands were initially 'web-shy,'" Barbara told me. "Most of them believed, 'This is not for us.' But we didn't think ignoring the net was a good option. For one thing, we knew that many of our guests were already on the web—using e-mail, looking for information on line, sometimes transacting too. We could see that a big sea change was happening and that it didn't make sense to ignore it. At the same time, we recognized the risks. So we asked ourselves, 'What would a Four Seasons experience on the web look like?' The question took us straight back to what guests knew and loved about the hotels: service designed around their needs, good value for money, and something else—beauty and comfort."

Barbara's marketing team knew there wasn't a magic formula for accomplishing their task. They were definitely in uncharted territory. So they decided to take two small initial steps that wouldn't box them into a specific direction and that would leave their options open. "We had this feeling that we needed to start out and just do something, and then learn as we went," Barbara told me.

At the time, most travel and hotel websites were primarily concerned with hooking people by giving them the best deals in the fewest clicks. Barbara's team opted to stress something very simple and very different—aesthetics. They set out to give customers a virtual preview of what staying in a Four Seasons would be like: relaxed, beautiful, and inspiring. As a result, the company's first website looked more like a magazine spread than a sales portal. Instead of flashing banners and blaring discount offers, it showcased a gallery of lush photographs and inviting write-ups about different Four Seasons properties. "We had always invested in high-quality photography for print materials," Barbara recalled. "So we looked at what we already had, and just moved it onto the web."

The next small step involved how to handle reservations and customer service. Most travel-related websites were pushing visitors to standardized reservation forms or FAQ pages in order to lower costs. But this approach felt completely out of step with Four Seasons' renowned emphasis on personalized service. "Booking engines at the time were unreliable and likely to waste a lot of the customer's time—two things that were completely incompatible with our guests' service expectations." So the team posted a new 800 reservations number on the site. That way, day or night, customers could interact with a live human being if and when they had questions or were ready to book their trip. The 800 number was a simple solution to an issue that could have derailed the entire website if they had gotten carried away with all of the various reservation and support options.

There were also no special "web rates." Until that time, Four Seasons guests had expected and received consistent retail rates no matter how they chose to make the reservation. That did not change in the online environment.

Within a few months, the first surprise occurred. The Four Seasons web team reported that visitors to the site were spending long periods of time clicking through the photographs and educating themselves about all the company's properties, and that many callers to the new 800 number were planning personal vacations rather than business trips. This data was quite unexpected, since historically business travelers had been the company's mainstay.

Surprise number two happened shortly after that. A leading Wall Street analyst issued a first-ever report comparing hotel web strategies. When it came to Four Seasons, his word-for-word comment still echoes loudly in Barbara's head today: "Spending time on the Four Seasons website makes us feel like we are already on vacation." The report was full of accolades, but it particularly applauded the site for its inspirational emphasis on leisure—something that really hadn't been the primary focus of the initial strategy!

At the same time all this was happening, Four Seasons was planning an exciting new expansion. Already recognized as the North American luxury hotel leader, the company was on a path to more than triple in the following decade—with new resorts and city hotels in global destinations. The timing could not have been better. "Everywhere you went in the world, people who valued quality were choosing the same brands—driving Mercedes or wearing Chanel," Barbara told me. "There was this huge preference for global brands of quality. And yet, there was really no such thing at the time in the hospitality industry. In their marketing strategies, many of these brands relied exclusively on print advertising and in-person sales. We used both, but clearly it was going to take much more." So the challenge was clear: Could Four Seasons use the Internet not just to bring new customers into the U.S. market but also as a tool to establish itself as the first branded worldwide player in luxury hospitality? Thanks to an innovative, step-by-step approach, they did just that.

First off, Barbara's team tailored the website to consumers who had already stayed with Four Seasons, or would want to. They created an online environment for people who loved to travel and did it often, for business and pleasure, and who wanted to inform themselves in depth—and be inspired, just as the Wall Street analyst had been. The site was enhanced to feature even more photographs and offer detailed information about things like room layouts and local activities. As booking engines improved, online reservation capability was added, but the 800 number remained in place, allowing guests to choose. Then, the content was translated into other languages—German and Japanese at first, since along with the United States, they were the largest global travel markets at the time. People responded. Within a few years, Four Seasons had gone from being the North American leader to being the leading internationally recognized symbol of hospitality excellence.

As the examples from Intuit, OneWorld Health, and Four Seasons show, surprises can reveal themselves in a variety of forms. Whether it's customer feedback, comments from taxi drivers, positive or negative industry events, successes or failures, or anything else that challenges our mindsets, surprises hold clues that can give us greater focus and direction.

Questions to Consider

- ⮑ Have you ever looked back at two or more seemingly unrelated experiences and realized they are connected?

- ⮑ What "small surprises" have you experienced that, when combined, had a much bigger implication due to the sum being much larger than the individual parts?

Surprising Ourselves Helps Us Surprise Others

Think back over your life and relive the moments when you were pleasantly surprised by what you might consider a breakthrough, possibly when you first experienced a new product or service or a way of doing business. Now, consider how those experiences made you *feel.* This isn't about crossing your legs, closing your eyes, and singing *Kumbaya* with your colleagues. But it is about getting in touch with who we are and what inspires us. Because the goal here isn't just to deliver positive surprises to customers—that's only part of the equation. If we want to create something that delivers wonder, delight, or that sense of exciting freshness that all great breakthroughs provide, one of the first steps is to find those things in ourselves.

I've asked people in all sorts of organizations about their surprises. Many eagerly share their experiences. But in some companies, I've received only catatonic stares in response to my questions. A lot of people don't like talking about times when they've been caught off guard. They think being surprised is a sign of weakness, something that should never happen, especially to powerful people in leadership positions. To concede that they were surprised about something means admitting they weren't in control—that they weren't successfully "managing." They're afraid that if they acknowledge their surprises others will see them as soft or incapable of leading.

The psychologist, Erich Fromm, noted this tendency when he said, "Once they are through the process of education, most people lose the capacity of wondering, of being surprised. They feel they ought to know everything, and hence that it is a sign of ignorance to be surprised or puzzled by anything." The real shame of this pervasive mindset is that it can prevent us from seeing the guideposts that can lie within surprises that, when seen, can reveal the best path to our ideal futures.

When we're surprised, we're prompted to question and potentially modify our mindsets, which can create greater clarity around a new opportunity or challenge. When this happens early on, it can help lead to big ideas, as we saw with SnapTax and OneWorld Health.

But it can also occur after we already know our future vision and direction, during the operational process of creating our breakthroughs, as the Four Seasons story demonstrated. In either case, new insights into what should be done and how to go about doing it are typically the result.

One of the ways to tap into the power of surprise is to continually ask ourselves provocative questions and then go beyond our comfort zones by exploring new areas and giving ourselves and our organizations new experiences. While it's important to proactively expand our perspectives on what's possible, it's also essential to remain keenly aware of how our values and assumptions influence our responses to the multitude of things that can occur when we're deeply involved in the inherently ambiguous process of creating breakthroughs.

Here's a review of some of the examples that have been presented to highlight the process of how surprises lead to shifts in mindsets that then produce greater strategic focus and inspired action:

- Gloria Montenegro de Chirouze started Caféotheque after being surprised by the poor quality of coffee in Paris. She realized that her long-standing appreciation of premium coffee could be transformed into a new business opportunity. She saw that she could help others become aspiring connoisseurs themselves if she could give them the same kind of coffee-drinking pleasure she derived herself.

- Scott Cook initially dismissed the fact that thousands of small businesses were using Quicken, which was designed for balancing personal checkbooks, not for the kind of debit accounting necessary for running a business. When he finally embraced this surprise, he discovered a huge market opportunity that led him to create QuickBooks, which transformed the small business accounting market and established Intuit as the undisputed market leader.

- Victoria Hale experienced a life-changing surprise in the form of a seemingly benign comment by a taxi driver. Hale's mindset instantly shifted, prompting her to question the fundamental business model underlying the entire pharmaceutical industry. As a result, she founded OneWorld Health, the first-ever nonprofit pharmaceutical company.

- Barbara Talbott and her team experienced two surprises during the process of building the Four Seasons website. The first involved their business customers' unexpected response to their early website, which revealed an untapped opportunity to promote leisure and vacations. The second surprise came in the form of a Wall Street analyst's report that jolted Barbara's marketing team into realizing that their newly minted website should become a key tool in helping the company extend into the global luxury market.

In all of these cases, real-world experiences led to a deeper recognition of personal motivations, outmoded assumptions, and new opportunities. With a change in awareness, these individuals and organizations transformed existing ways of doing business or trail-blazed entirely new paths. The next six chapters describe how to navigate the dynamics of business breakthroughs and how to harness the power of surprise in the process.

Questions to Consider

➲ What surprises have you had that resulted in greater personal or business clarity?

➲ How did these surprises challenge your assumptions or increase your awareness of a challenge or opportunity?

➲ What did you start doing differently as a result?

3

Leapfrogging to Breakthroughs

A journey is like marriage. The certain way to be wrong is to think you control it.

—John Steinbeck

Chapter Three Key Messages

1. Creating business breakthroughs is a journey.
2. New mindsets are needed, not just new tools.
3. Surprises often join us on our journeys.

Mehmood Khan, Chief Scientific Officer at PepsiCo, is responsible for the company's research and development, including extending the business beyond its traditional products such as Pepsi, Gatorade, and Doritos. Mehmood's achievements are many. He helped re-launch Gatorade by introducing a variety of new products with cutting-edge sports performance-focused ingredients. He has also begun creating a whole new line of "good for you" snack foods that represent the biggest future thrust for the company. And yet, as much as Mehmood has accomplished, in talking with him, it's clear that he still sees his mission and PepsiCo's future as a work in progress, a challenging trek full of twists, turns, ups, downs, and—yes—surprises along the way. "Big things take time to take hold," he said to me. "We're making it clear to everyone that it's OK not to freak out if things take time. Things will happen we can't anticipate and where we'll experience both successes and failures. This is all part of it."

Mehmood's comments reinforce something that I've seen over and over again and that was discussed by many of the people I spoke with during the course of writing this book—that the journey to breakthroughs involves much more than just finding and capitalizing on something surprising. Of course every breakthrough looks different and involves a unique set of challenges and experiences. The journey may take longer for some than for others. It may be tougher for some than for others. And it may yield different forms of recognition and reward.

Any journey through uncertainty and ambiguity may include large and small surprises. But while surprises can become assets when they happen, leapfrogging to breakthroughs is a *process*, not a one-time event. The goal is to approach the steps along the paths to our breakthroughs as mini-destinations in themselves, which can help us get through the tough times, capitalize on our successes, and continue moving forward to realize the larger prize.

New Mindsets Are the Missing Link

When it comes to big ideas, I've come across two types of organizations. Leaders inside the first type tell me they're searching for the inspiration that will transform their business. They feel stuck in their rut and say they need to push their thinking to reveal the new ingredients for breakthrough success—the products, services, strategies, and processes that will allow them to serve up a big new opportunity. In the second type of organization, I hear leaders lamenting the opposite problem. "We have lots of ideas," they say to me, "but we just can't get traction with any of them." These organizations may already have many of their ingredients, but they still need to find their recipes for success.

Over the last ten years, I've seen more and more organizations struggling to find bigger and better ideas—and the formulas for making them real—so that they can have a greater positive impact. Their leaders are incredibly intelligent people who possess a solid grasp of the latest and greatest business theories, models, and tools. They've read all the books out there. They've attended all the right conferences. And yet, when I speak to them, I feel their frustration and their yearning for a level of personal and organizational success that goes far beyond where they are today. They know something's missing, but they can't pinpoint it.

A lot of great books have been written about topics related to breakthroughs, and they include many useful concepts like "tipping points,"[28] "blue oceans,"[29] and "disruptive innovations."[30] As a result, we now have a pretty good grasp of the external success factors and tools—tracking industry trends, uncovering or anticipating unmet customer needs, and creating new business models—that can help us stake claim to new opportunities and markets. When I talk to many leaders, however, they still struggle to get their arms around the seemingly elusive leadership success factors involved in negotiating the often-messy journey that Mehmood described so eloquently.

The ironic thing is that there's also an overabundance of resources out there today that provide prescriptive step-by-step models and approaches for creative thinking, strategic innovation, and transformational change. But there's one problem with the approach many take: Creating breakthroughs is not about following a recipe. Far from it. When we seek formulaic certainty, we can lose sight of the underlying mindsets that are actually the most important critical success factors—the things that allow us to remain flexible, agile, and optimistically persistent during times of great uncertainty.

One of the toughest things about writing this book was trying to put an incredibly complex, fluid, and dynamic process into a structured framework supported by practical tools. Even in today's sound-bite world that's all about silver bullets and magic pills, the worst thing I could wish upon any leader or organization is that they take a model—yes, even mine!—and create a linear, step-by-step process out of it with the intention of getting a breakthrough. I know many of us want tried-and-true "best practices." And for most of my own professional life, I too have sought out repeatable processes and proven methodologies. While this book provides some pretty specific recommendations on techniques to use and things to do, one of the things I've come to learn is that if we're going to be successful in today's ever-changing business environment, we need to take best practices with a grain of salt and instead look to "best principles" to guide our unique efforts.

With all this in mind, I've come up with an overarching framework that I call the *leapfrogging life cycle*. Let me be clear: This is not a step-by-step how-to guide. But it does outline the key phases and dynamics that characterize the process of leading business breakthroughs. The chapters following this one delve into each phase of the life cycle in detail and provide practical discussion questions, activities, and tools that can be adapted and applied to any type of organization.

The Journey to Breakthroughs Involves Distinct Phases

The leapfrogging life cycle traces the path to breakthroughs by describing the leadership and organizational dynamics involved at various phases over time. The truth is that achieving breakthrough business success is a dynamic process that can't be "managed" in the traditional sense. A lot of trial and error goes into it. Success often depends on how well we address the "soft stuff"—how we deal with uncertainty and ambiguity, how engaged and invested we are personally, how we deal with both small setbacks and large failures, and how we respond to surprises.

The leapfrogging life cycle quite literally depicts the ups and downs involved in creating breakthroughs. In the coming chapters, I'll present a number of real-life examples and supporting research studies to bring each of these phases to life. For now, here's a brief overview of what occurs in each:

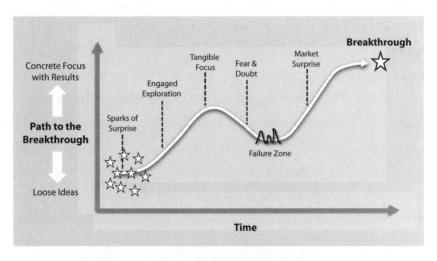

The Leapfrogging Life Cycle

Sparks of Surprise   Breakthroughs often start with "Sparks of Surprise"—initial insights into a need, problem, or opportunity area that deeply resonate with our interests, values, and motivations. This leads us to question our long-held assumptions or realize that there might just be a better way to do things. At this early stage we usually don't yet have a specific idea or solution; we just sense that "something big is out there" that we're compelled to better understand and define.

Engaged Exploration   With a new conviction of purpose, we go out into the world with excitement. Our curiosity engages us in a way that compels us to explore new areas beyond our day-to-day routine. Through this "Engaged Exploration," we learn everything we can about the problems, needs, challenges, requirements, and gaps pertaining to our area of interest. When we put ourselves into situations that push us beyond our comfort zone, we often experience surprises that challenge our existing mental models. When this happens, our eyes open up to a whole host of possible new directions.

Tangible Focus   Our exploration teaches us new things, which helps us to arrive at a new level of insight. With a sense of the true nature of our breakthrough, now it's time to put some solid stakes into the ground to make it real. As we move forward, the steps we take to bring our breakthroughs to life can result in further surprises. These surprises continue to challenge our assumptions and help us hone in on what, exactly, we need to create and how best to do it. I call this new level of insight "Tangible Focus."

How can "focus" be "tangible"? After all, at this early stage we're still desperately trying to "sculpt fog." I don't mean that the focus can be touched in the physical sense. I simply mean that we've achieved a firmer grasp of our subject area. Our focus may be in the form of a hard conclusion or just hunches and hypotheses. It's during this phase that all of our excitement and learning coalesce into a solid sense of direction that's grounded in real action.

Fear and Doubt (and the Failure Zone)   Now that we've put a mental stake into the ground, so to speak, we see things differently. We look at problems, needs, challenges, requirements, or gaps through a new lens. But as we move forward, outline solutions, and test our ideas, we realize that many of our initial thoughts and assumptions were only partly correct and need to be revised. As it becomes clear that a lot of hard work lies ahead, and that the answers we're looking for are far from clear-cut, we question what we're doing. Our initial enthusiasm starts to wane. Fear and doubt set in. We enter what I call the "Failure Zone," the graveyard of a million potential breakthroughs.

The reason many people fail at this point isn't a matter of ability, but mindset. It's not that we can't overcome the challenges or get the work done. It's because we simply give up. We aren't prepared to let go of the status quo and embrace the realm of ambiguity and uncertainty. I've seen it play out this way time and time again. But I've also seen plenty of people persist to push through the failure zone. And that's when the really good stuff starts to happen.

Market Surprise   Those who forge on don't always achieve instant success, but they do start to experience wins that provide rewards in the form of additional learning, positive feedback, and results. They adapt and modify their approaches. And, as they do so, they gain greater motivation to persevere. Others begin to recognize the value of the new solution or approach. The wins begin to snowball and the market starts to experience the positive surprise associated with the breakthrough first hand. This generates broader interest and buzz, which build momentum and accelerate the journey to the breakthrough.

L E A P S		Strategy
L	Listen	Start with yourself, not the market
E	Explore	Go outside to stretch the inside
A	Act	Take small simple steps, again and again and again
P	Persist	Take the surprise out of failure
S	Seize	Make the journey part of the (surprising) destination

The LEAPS Model

I want to emphasize again that the leapfrogging life cycle is admittedly a gross simplification of what can be an incredibly complex process. In reality, there are fits, starts, highs, lows, successes, and failures in each phase of the life cycle. Some of these phases overlap and can even repeat themselves, which creates cycles within the life cycle. But I'm a strong believer that simplicity is the antidote to complexity. To this end, I've created the acronym LEAPS that highlights specific things leaders can do to find insight, direction, and the strength to successfully navigate each phase of the leapfrogging life cycle themselves, and with their teams and organizations.

The LEAPS model maps to the leapfrogging life cycle by providing guidance and tools to successfully address the dynamics within each life cycle phase. The linkages are shown in the figure at the top of page 59.

Surprises Often Join Us on Our Journeys

First and foremost, the leapfrogging life cycle is intended to outline the overall process of leading business breakthroughs. While by now

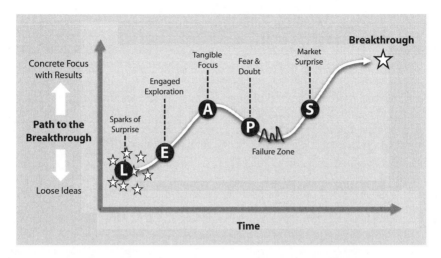

LEAPS Model Mapped to the Leapfrogging Life Cycle

it should be pretty evident that the power of surprise is a key theme in this book, I want to emphasize that not every phase of the leapfrogging life cycle is necessarily laden with surprises. But, uncertainty and ambiguity are ever-present throughout the process of creating breakthroughs, and because of this, surprises can show up anywhere and at any time—and it's helpful to be ready for them.

In the following chapters I'll review each phase of the leapfrogging life cycle in detail. I'll bring the leapfrogging process to life through a variety of examples, some from organizations you'll recognize and others that will likely be new to you. I'll show you how to use the power of surprise to let go of things, uncover things, and create things—and I'll show you how to challenge assumptions and overcome the barriers that create artificial boundaries and limit possibilities. I'll also provide questions and exercises that you can use to jump-start the leapfrogging process for yourself and in your own organization.

4

Listen:
Start with Yourself,
Not the Market

*No question is so difficult to answer as that to which
the answer is obvious.*

—*George Bernard Shaw*

Chapter Four Key Messages

1. Holistic thinking reveals the biggest opportunities.

2. Our fundamental strengths provide threads to the future.

3. Breakthroughs begin with ourselves, not the market.

Think of the biggest assignment you've had. Now multiply the difficulty level of that task by at least three or four times. That will probably give you an idea of what Tina Christopoulou was facing a few years back.

Tina had to create five-year "roadmaps" for every business in the Colgate-Palmolive Corporation. We all know Colgate for its toothpaste. But the company also churns out dozens of different products, everything from deodorant to bathroom cleaner to fabric conditioner to shower gel. And Tina was responsible for coming up with a plan for how each of these lines should grow and evolve—not just in the United States, but globally. Nothing of this breadth, depth, and scale had ever been attempted before at the company.

I was brought in to help Tina figure out the best way to approach this mother of all business plans. The first thing we did was schedule a series of interviews with top-level executives from all of Colgate's major divisions. Just about everyone we spoke to said the same thing: They weren't sure they had enough knowledge about their customers' product needs, preferences, and desires to create the plans. We left these discussions in a tailspin since we needed this information for the very first planning meeting. Normally, the next move of a big company like Colgate would be to commission a ton of market research to fill in the gaps. But Tina's deadline was just too tight for that to happen. So, instead of going out and collecting brand-new data, we put together a small team to extract every shred of already-existing research they could find within the company.

Tina and I hoped that if we looked hard enough, we could unearth all of the information we needed. We were right—or at least we thought we were. By the start of the executive meetings, we had uncovered more than 250 studies focused on all of Colgate's global product lines. Not only that, but we had synthesized the data into several very impressive presentations. We were pleased with the results of our detective work, and we assumed that our findings would blow everyone away. But what came next blew *us* away.

Put bluntly, during the first planning meeting we learned that our slickly packaged reports could have been put to use as placemats for the lunch spread. We just didn't need them. The team members in attendance already knew way more about their consumers than any of the research studies we had found. Pretty much everyone—from

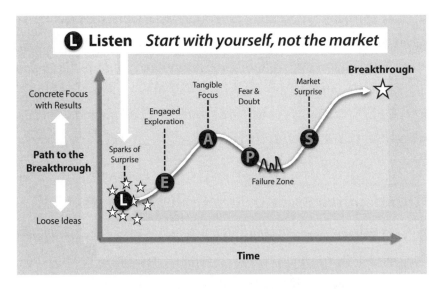

Listen Phase of the Leapfrogging Life Cycle

Tina and me to the executives we interviewed to many of the team members themselves—had underestimated the resident knowledge that existed, which in many cases went far beyond what we had unearthed during our research gathering.

Team members from Asia told us that Japanese women were interested in soap that whitens skin and that Chinese consumers believed that toothpaste and mouthwash could help regulate body temperature. Latin American teams reported that people in Mexico wanted household cleaners that work on cement, since it's the most common flooring material in the region. Meanwhile, we heard that American teenagers were looking for products with more natural ingredients and that European consumers were in the market for a fabric softener specifically designed for air-dried clothing. The list went on and on.

My experience with Tina forms the basis of this chapter's core message: *We already possess what we need to gain clarity on our greatest opportunities*. We all have what we need right now—ourselves, our teams, and our organizations—we just need to listen to them in the right ways. Contrary to conventional wisdom, the goal is to uncover insight and direction from within ourselves as the starting point, not to look to customers and the market for them. This chapter describes why and how to do it.

Liberating the Brain Delivers the Big Picture

I often work with organizations that have spent huge sums of money on consultants, researchers, and third-party reports in order to uncover new opportunities. The results are always quite impressive—beautiful PowerPoint presentations, video clips of focus groups, and spreadsheets that only trained statisticians can understand. Yet time and again I hear these fateful words from the organizations' business leaders: "We have the *what*, but we just can't get to the *so what*." In other words, they've got data up the proverbial wazoo, but turning all that information into fresh ideas and actionable opportunities is a different matter.

During the Colgate roadmapping meetings, once we realized how knowledgeable the team members already were, we switched our entire approach from focusing on the *what* to the *so what*. Tina asked participants to come to the sessions ready to share their knowledge and insights—not through PowerPoint presentations or ready-made reports but through impromptu conversations. They had to prepare for the meetings, but they had to do it in their heads. And they had to be ready to talk through their ideas in real time. To get them in the right mindset, we asked them broad questions like, What are the biggest problems, gaps, and challenges for Colgate's customers today? In short, we asked people to "liberate their brains"—to take a huge step back from all the details and to look instead at the overarching patterns or the *so what*.

Under Tina's guidance, the meetings became a series of intense but informal discussions. Participants represented their own group's knowledge and interests, but they did so in the spirit of contributing to a holistic picture of larger Colgate opportunities. They found commonalities and highlighted differences across countries and cultures. They prioritized consumers' needs. And they identified technologies, research directions, products, services, and strategies that they believed could be real breakthroughs.

By the end of the meetings, Tina was brimming with confidence and new ideas to bring to her road maps. Today, her project is seen as a major contributor to Colgate's product strategies around the world. And as a by-product of the process, it also helped build the organization's widespread appreciation for global, cross-functional collaboration.

Tina's experience can teach us something valuable. Contrary to conventional wisdom, robust research, detailed analysis, and overly rational thinking can actually get in the way of identifying big breakthrough opportunities. When we load ourselves down with the *what*, it's impossible to decipher the *so what* lurking under the surface. And that's good news because it means that when we're getting started, we don't necessarily have to spend time or money doing tons of market research, conducting detailed competitive analyses, or assessing technologies. It's also good news because putting analysis on the back burner helps avoid information overload that can paralyze decision making.

If you're having a heart attack right now just thinking about bypassing market research in preparation for your next big breakthrough, you're probably not alone. If it's any consolation, some of the most innovative companies in the world don't do market research at all. Steve Jobs, the late CEO of Apple, once said in an interview, "We do no market research. We don't hire consultants. The only consultants I've ever hired in my 10 years is one firm to analyze Gateway's retail strategy so I would not make some of the same mistakes they made [when launching Apple's retail stores]."[31]

The retailer Target has had a similar philosophy. Robyn Waters, former Vice President of Trend, Design and Product Development at Target, recently told me the same thing. Robyn said that Bob Ulrich, former CEO of Target, was adamantly opposed to most direct consumer market research, especially focus groups. During Target's breakthrough growth years, they used their own instincts to infuse leading-edge design into everything they did, from transforming the stores' layout to creating partnerships with world-renowned designers like Philippe Starck—which ultimately led to transforming the retailer from "Target" into the "Tar-jay" that many of us recognize today as the leader in just about everything "cheap chic."

For many, it's difficult to put aside the culturally ingrained idea that we need to do a bunch of structured research and analyses as our first step. Some may consider the opposite of analysis or analytical decision making as simply using intuition or tapping into gut instincts. But it's not such an either-or decision. I'm not talking about neglecting our rational minds—just restraining our natural tendency to analyze everything to death, while liberating the other side of our brains. Here's some research that explains what I mean.

Imagine you're asked to compare four different apartment listings. Each has a set of twelve bullets points describing their respective features; in all, there are forty-eight different pieces of information you need to consider. Apartments differ in size, they have different amenities, and some are in slightly better neighborhoods. One apartment has a landlord who isn't very friendly but some of its other features are quite positive. You're asked to select the "best" apartment of the four.

What you don't know is that two researchers from the University of Amsterdam, Ap Dijksterhuis and Loran Nordgren, have intentionally skewed the apartment listings so that one apartment has the most desirable features, one has predominantly negative features, and two are somewhere in between. In addition, their study has three groups of participants. Participants in the first group are asked to select the best apartment immediately after reading the comparisons; they are not given enough time to really think about their choice. The other two groups are allowed a three-minute break in between viewing the apartment listings and making their selection. Of these two groups, one is instructed to review the listings and ponder their answer during the three-minute interlude. The other group, however, is distracted with another activity during the three minutes prior to naming the most desirable apartment. Which group do you think picks the best apartment most often?

Dijksterhuis and Nordgren have conducted this and similar experiments using the subjects of apartments, roommates, and cars many times.[32] Their findings are always the same. The third group—the one that's distracted with the irrelevant activity—consistently chooses the most desirable apartment. The reason for this is simple. The seemingly intrusive distraction actually gives them valuable "unconscious thinking time" to evaluate their options without even being aware that they are doing so. In other words, they're processing the glut of data subconsciously. This is pretty interesting stuff in itself, but there's more.

The researchers also found that these unconscious thinkers were better able to cluster and categorize the large amounts of information given to them, such as the laundry lists of bullet points describing the apartments. When asked about their thought processes, they reported that they used holistic judgment (a feeling for the big picture) in making their decisions, versus the other participants who tended to base their choices on weighing trade-offs among only a few of the data points.

This research tells us two important things related to leapfrogging. First, unconscious thinking can be a great source of insight. During unconscious thinking, our brains essentially work behind the scenes to synthesize data and draw conclusions without us even knowing it. This is why we'll often hear someone tell us to "sleep on it," which basically means give your brain a rest and let the answer come naturally. We all have access to this hidden source of untapped innovation, but for most of us it's not our go-to resource. Again, I'm not saying that there isn't a valuable role for analytical thinking—it's just not the thing to emphasize on the front end of the leapfrogging process.

When we are under stress or trying to solve a pressing problem, we tend to rev up our brains into overdrive. The thought of setting the work aside for a time seems counterproductive. But it might just be the best thing to do. One of the most effective decisions Tina made during her Colgate roadmapping meetings, for example, was to give the participants ample rest periods between sessions. This downtime gave them valuable space for unconscious thinking and it helped foster their holistic viewpoints.

Second, this research also tells us something about finding patterns to uncover opportunities. When we try to hold large amounts of information in our heads—like all the trends, customer needs, competitive activity, and so on going on in an industry, or even multiple industries—we simply can't process such complexity with what we've got between our ears. The patterns and themes that represent opportunities can more easily be discovered using a broad brush that reveals the overall challenges or latent needs of the market, stakeholders, or business situation. When we find ourselves staring at a lot of data, statistics, or mind-numbing charts and graphs, we've taken a step too far into the analysis zone. The goal is to seek big conclusions, the top-line insights that provide overall direction, versus details that will leave us drowning in data. Letting one's unconscious mind take over can help to separate the wheat from the chaff by allowing us to surprise ourselves with what we already know—just like a signal flare popping up to reveal a breakthrough that's been there all along but has been hiding in plain sight.

Tina's road mapping initiative at Colgate was so successful because it did most of the things I just described. People came to the sessions ready to share their ideas and knowledge that had been percolating between sessions. While they were given a structure to guide discussions and create the project's deliverables, the expectation was that any information brought into the room would be shared as a natural part of the conversation and would not be constrained by pre-made PowerPoints (a breakthrough in itself for many companies!). Similarly, Apple's and Target's rejection of market research shows how their starting point wasn't based in data but rather a holistic, multidimensional view of the world.

Questions to Consider

- ⇨ In what instances have you looked at data when you would be better served by seeking overall patterns and themes within the bigger picture?

- ⇨ What information do you already possess about your industry, customers, markets, competitors, and stakeholders? What's the *so what* of all this data?

➲ What are the big top-line conclusions you can make that give you a sense of the overall opportunity or direction?

➲ What can you do to slow down in order to step back from all the details and noise so you can find meaningful connections and opportunities?

Fundamental Strengths Are Threads to the Future

When we are staring at the world of possibilities, it's easy to forget what we know when we're overwhelmed by what we don't know. The goal is to balance this natural tension by maintaining a solid sense of our existing strengths while at the same time recognizing where we need to push ourselves in new directions. This isn't to say we must draw on only our existing technologies, products, or processes. But we do need to understand our starting point from the perspective of what really gives us our core identity, including where we excel today and where we believe we can excel in the future.

Before the success of Apple's iPod, many had criticized the company for its "closed" approach. Unlike Microsoft, which licensed Windows to PC manufacturers, Apple kept its operating system proprietary, so that the only place you could get an Apple computer was from Apple itself. This strategy ultimately limited Apple's distribution and stifled its growth. Now, even with today's focus on making apps on its iPhones and iPads widely available from other developers, many of the same principles from the early years that almost killed the company are actually at the heart of its success today.

Steve Jobs once said that the reason so many people want to work at Apple is because "You can't do what you can do at Apple anywhere else." He went on to say, "The engineering is long gone in most PC companies. In the consumer electronics companies, they don't understand the software parts of it. And so you really can't make the products that you can make at Apple anywhere else right now. Apple's the only company that has everything under one roof."[33] Apple's ability to stay true to its strengths and build on them—despite the great challenges it once experienced using very similar approaches—is the basis for its latest breakthroughs in smartphones, tablet computers, apps, and entertainment. It's also how it continues to engage its employees and prospective workers who are lining up at the door wanting to work for the company.

Here's another example from a much lesser known company than Apple, but one that demonstrates how recognizing your knowledge and skills can lead to surprising new opportunities. This story is about real estate.

Location, location, location is the old real estate adage. Every builder wants that pristine lot with the view or that premier business spot with tons of foot traffic, right? Not necessarily.

Ohio property developer Todd Davis pays attention to location too. But what he's looking for is a little unorthodox. What do I mean by unorthodox? Well, one of his company's biggest scores in recent years was purchasing an abandoned auto parts factory with crumbling, asbestos-filled walls. Another winner for Davis was landing the rights to build on an old soda ash production facility complete with hundreds of acres of contaminated soil.

Needless to say, Davis didn't have to win bidding wars for these deals. Not many buyers were eager to get their hands on them. But for Davis and his team at Hemisphere Development, these so-called "brownfields" were bona fide pay dirt. The dilapidated automotive factory is on its way to becoming a gleaming new casino and resort. And the old soda ash site will soon be a bucolic colony of residential and commercial neighborhoods connected by scenic hiking trails.

Davis began his brownfield work as a young lawyer in a large law firm, where he got a clear view of just how troublesome old industrial sites can be for everyone involved. Local governments lose millions in tax revenues when factories and other commercial centers shut down. The owners of the sites face gargantuan fines and huge costs to clean them up. Neighboring communities have to deal with contamination, job loss, and blighted buildings. Worst of all, even though no one wants these eyesores to stay the way they are, they rarely get turned into something else. The costs and the hassles are just too daunting.

But Davis saw the gleam of opportunity in all that gloom. State and federal agencies began to offer generous grants and tax incentives to anyone willing to turn these industrial no-man's lands into productive properties again. Davis realized that someone with his expertise, and his unique willingness to plod through dense thickets of political and regulatory obstacles, could help revitalize communities and make a nice financial return in the process. "Brownfield developers are sometimes perceived like modern day gunfighters," Davis told a congressional committee in 2005. "Riding into town, wearing a white hat, providing the intellectual muscle, creativity and capital to tackle a community's brownfield needs."[34] Davis possessed all of these things, and he knew he could apply these assets to this emerging opportunity.

Early on, Davis recognized that his unique problem-solving skills, creative thinking, and unwavering persistence were exactly the traits required to corral and manage the complex ecosystem of stakeholders involved in moving brownfield projects from conception through to fruition. Through this lens, he realized that a new model could be created to flip the definition of "prime" real estate. While most others look at contaminated properties as nightmare liabilities, Davis sees them as bargain-basement opportunities. Over the years,

Davis has mastered this complex process of brownfield orchestration. He's literally written the book on it. Put out by the American Bar Association, his *Comprehensive Guide to Redeveloping Contaminated Property* has become the bible of a burgeoning new industry.

Every individual, team, and organization possesses a unique blend of knowledge, experience, and human and technological capabilities. By considering our most fundamental strengths, we can shift our lens in a way that often gives us insight into new opportunities that we're uniquely positioned to lead.

Questions to Consider

➲ What are you really great at doing?

➲ What are the skills and abilities that allow you to do these things?

➲ What are the most fundamental benefits that you currently or could provide (be sure to think more deeply than just your products or services)?

➲ What unique combinations of individual, team, or organizational strengths can give you a leg up to create something new or bypass the competition?

Breakthroughs Begin with Ourselves, Not the Market

Breakthroughs are self-serving. In the marketing and product development world, it's generally heresy to suggest that you should innovate for yourself rather than beginning with research into customer needs. The assumption is that the needs and wants of customers should be the sole catalyst for every innovation. But starting with ourselves is exactly what to do when going for breakthroughs. Just to clarify, this doesn't mean we should ignore customers; we just need to kick things off from a slightly different starting point.

Going back to Apple for a moment, Steve Jobs didn't create the first Macintosh computer because a group of market researchers told him that people wanted a new-fangled desktop computer that could be controlled by a mouse. He did it because he simply felt compelled to create it. Even the minor details in the Mac arose from his prior personal experience combined with an inner desire to make something that would be seen and experienced as truly elegant. For example, Jobs included the various serif and sans serif font types—that became so closely associated with the Mac and ultimately most computers—because he had learned about them in a calligraphy course he took after he dropped out of his regular courses in college. In referencing his calligraphy background, Jobs once said, "None of this had even a hope of any practical application in my life. But ten years later, when we were designing the first Macintosh computer, it all came back to me. And we designed it all into the Mac. It was the first computer with beautiful typography."[35] Jobs and his colleagues at Apple realized there was a big gap and market need because they felt it themselves. They "knew" there was an opportunity because they themselves wanted to be their own first customers.

Just imagine having to work on something big, uncertain, and extremely challenging that you don't care about at all for yourself—something that really doesn't have a lot of connection or meaning to your interests or life. Under these circumstances, going the extra mile would probably be pretty tough. But when you're doing it for yourself, it's another story.

When Nora Pouillon first came to the United States from Austria in the 1960s, she was appalled by the typical American's diet: canned vegetables, hormone-laden meat, tasteless fruit, and processed meals with unpronounceable ingredients. Nothing matched the freshness and taste that she was used to on the farm where she grew up and that she longed to experience again. As a homemaker, she started to cook simple, healthy food for herself and her family. But what started as a personal passion soon developed into a business mission. In 1979, Pouillon opened Restaurant Nora in Washington, DC. From the start, Nora was not just another restaurant. Calling it a sociological experiment—or even a pipedream—might be more apt. At least that's how most of Pouillon's peers in the industry saw it, because she was determined to use exclusively organic ingredients, most of them locally grown. These days, that's standard practice for many upscale eateries. But in 1979, talking about seasonal, locally grown organic food was like talking about cheese sliced from the surface of the moon.

Pouillon quite literally had to cook up her business model from scratch. Unlike most chefs, she couldn't just pick up a phone and fill her pantry by ordering from wholesalers. She had to go to the sources: the fields and stables themselves. Amish and Mennonite farmers had been growing organic food in the region for decades, so they were some of her first suppliers. But for many of the ingredients she planned to use, organic options did not exist yet, so she had to talk other local farmers into producing them.

The results of Pouillon's hard work were immediate and, well, groundbreaking. Restaurant Nora took off. And why wouldn't it? Have you ever tasted the difference between a bland, store-bought tomato and one picked straight from the vine? That was pretty much the difference between Nora's fare and what you could find at every other restaurant. Pouillon was reintroducing the American palate to the taste of fresh, high-quality food. And people liked it. A lot.

"To have a good quality of life, you have to pay attention to what you surround yourself with and what you put in your body. . . . I am an advocate for sustainable living," Pouillon once said.[36] And

she practices what she preaches, which is why *Fitness* magazine recognized Pouillon as one of the healthiest chefs in America. Establishing Restaurant Nora gave Pouillon the opportunity to provide
herself with the elements of a sustainable lifestyle she couldn't find
when she first came to the United States—and it is now a thriving
business that gives others a taste of what's possible.

Like Steve Jobs and the team at Apple, Nora Pouillon didn't begin her venture by conducting research or analyzing customer needs.
She started with a simple but burning desire to make a difference—for
herself and her family, and for others. Oftentimes it's a personal experience that leads to a new insight about the world, something that's
broken, something that should ideally exist but doesn't, a big gap in a
process or procedure, or some type of social injustice. Whatever the
focus, the solution that results provides dual meaning; it addresses the
needs or motivations of the leader, team, or organization while at the
same time satisfying the unmet desires of the market.

Questions to Consider

➲ What are examples of experiences from which you gained a new
insight, realized something was broken, or found a big gap that
you wanted to fix? What did you learn?

➲ Where do you want to make a real difference? In what ways do
you want things to change for yourself and for others? How do
your interests and motivations tie into your business goals?

➲ In what ways can you add a greater sense of purpose and
broader contribution to what you do? Where are opportunities
to do something that provides dual meaning—deeper meaning
both for yourself and for those you serve?

➲ What can you do to become an evangelist for your cause?
How can you educate others, write the "bible" for your field, or

establish yourself as an expert—not to fuel your ego but because it's a means to your greater end?

Making It Real

We've talked about why liberating our brains is important for sifting through the noise to identify the bigger needs and opportunities. We've looked at how breakthroughs are tied to what we already do and know. And we've explored why it's important to listen to ourselves first before shifting our focus outward.

The goal of the first phase of the leapfrogging process is to find general direction and focus, not to nail down all the details and plans. Once we have a sense of direction, we can do things to gain even greater clarity and fill in the details. This is what I'll describe in the next chapter. It's also why iteration—going back to revisit a previous step—is often a part of the leapfrogging process, since as we learn more and update our assumptions, we gain further clarity on our own motivations and the specific things that will lead us closer to our breakthrough. Here are some specific things you can begin doing now to find your own sparks of personal surprise.

Leapfrogging Tools

1. Find Surprise in What You Already Know

Give your team an assignment to come together in work sessions and answer some or all of the questions posed in this chapter. Consider starting with these questions about liberating your brain:

- In what ways have you been looking at and responding to detailed data when you'd be better served by stepping back and seeking overall patterns and themes of the bigger picture?

- What data do you possess about your industry, customers, markets, competitors, and stakeholders?

- What's the *so what* of all this data?

- What are the big top-line conclusions you can make that give you a sense of overall opportunity or direction?

Provide your team with these questions before the work session and tell them they need to be prepared to discuss their answers verbally. Take notes during the session and send them out immediately following the meeting.

Give the team additional questions at the end of the session in preparation for the next meeting. For example, ask them to seek out stories from across the organization that highlight your strengths. Ask them to find examples of when you delighted a customer, exceeded financial targets, introduced a breakthrough innovation, or did something remarkable. When you get back together, share the stories and then find themes from these examples by extracting those things that led to these successes and are at the heart of what you do best. Use common language when describing your strengths so that anyone, even your grandmother, can understand what you're talking about (no technobabble!). Then ask: How can we combine or build on our strengths to tap into new opportunities?

Modify this activity by including other questions and exercises from this chapter. Work in intense bursts, taking time between sessions, from a few days to a couple of weeks.

2. Look at Customers' Causes

Think about where your customers are focused on contributing to higher causes—things they care about deeply and are doing something about themselves. How can you tie into this greater sense of purpose for your own organization?

3. Uncover Driving Motivations

Consider where you really want to make a big difference in the world—for customers, for your industry, or for your organization. Think about the problems you want to fix, the gaps you want to fill, or the contributions you want to make. Think about what would have to happen for you to be able to deliver something of great magnitude: What would it look like? Who would it affect? What value would it deliver and to whom? How would it provide benefit back to the organization?

4. Jump to the Top Line

Convene a cross-functional, multidisciplinary group and discuss the big trends, needs, and challenges in your industry or market. Don't worry about the details. Go for top-line insights. Ask questions like the ones Tina Christopoulou from Colgate asked her team: What are the biggest problems, gaps, and challenges of customers today? What new benefits could we deliver that would make the greatest difference to them? What can we do or provide that will be radically different from what else is out there in the market? Tell people to prepare, but to bring only themselves and their existing knowledge, not their PowerPoints!

5

Explore:
Go Outside to
Stretch the Inside

*The harder you fight to hold on to specific assumptions,
the more likely there's gold in letting go of them.*

—*John Seely Brown*

Chapter Five Key Messages

1. We can see our assumptions only after we overcome them.

2. Expanding our perspective softens our mindsets.

3. Pushing beyond the limits of our comfort zones leads to
   new insights.

4. Empathy leads to surprise.

I have a quick story for you and then a question. First the story: A
bus driver was heading down Van Ness Avenue in my hometown of
San Francisco. He went through a stop sign without even slowing
down, then turned onto a one-way street going the opposite direction as the rest of the traffic. A police officer saw the whole thing,
but he didn't stop the bus driver or issue a ticket because no laws had
been broken. How can this scenario be possible?

If you answered that the bus driver was *walking down the street*, you are correct. This is a very simple example to illustrate how we all make assumptions. Most people just assume that a bus driver is always driving a bus. But, of course, that's not the case. The most important part of this exercise isn't to point out that an assumption may have been made in the first place—it's only natural to do so. It's to show that most of us recognize that we've made an assumption only *after* we've discovered that our thinking was invalid or that it led us astray. And by then, it can often be "too late."

Yes, it's a paradox: We can't see our most fundamental assumptions until we successfully overcome them. This means that we can really understand the mindsets and barriers that once stood in our way only retrospectively—by looking back on them after the fact.

Let's go back to the bus driver for a moment. What if I had framed things in the scenario a little differently and included another statement up front: "In San Francisco, people use cars, take the bus, or

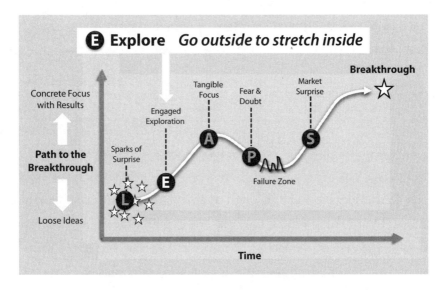

Explore Phase of the Leapfrogging Life Cycle

walk down the street to get where they're going." How would this have affected your assumptions? For most people, the idea that it's possible the bus driver could be walking down the street would have been planted in their brains as they read the rest of the scenario—and they would have more easily overcome their limiting assumption that bus drivers only drive buses. When leapfrogging, the goal is to continually broaden our perspective so that we can overcome our assumptions *before* they limit our options or slow us down.

This little prelude leads us to the core concept of this chapter: *Our limiting mindsets are invisible until we overcome them, which we can do through venturing outside of our comfort zones.*

Expanding Our Perspective Softens Our Mindsets

Adam Galinsky and William Maddux recently conducted a series of experiments[37] that reveal some of the benefits of pushing past the boundaries of our existing mindsets. These university researchers looked at the differences between people who have lived in two or more countries versus those who have never lived outside their country of origin.

In one of their studies, Galinsky and Maddux took 108 people and paired them up in teams of two. Each of the fifty-four teams was asked to negotiate the sale of a fictitious gas station. In each team, one person played the role of the buyer and one was the seller. Prior to the experiment, the researchers told the buyers that they needed to purchase the gas station from their partner, but that they could spend only *up to a specific amount*, and no more. Sellers were told they needed to sell their gas station but they *couldn't accept anything lower than a specified amount*. Both buyers and sellers remained unaware that they were set up: The maximum purchase price given to the buyers was less than the lowest amount the sellers were told they could accept. Thus, because the sale price was the single and only issue presented to the teams for negotiation, there was a huge barrier inherent in the scenario that could quickly produce a stalemate.

But the researchers also provided a potential way out. They gave people some additional information to create the possibility that the pairs might find some shared interests during their negotiation. The buyers, for example, were told in advance that they would need to hire managers to run their stations once they purchased them. And the sellers were told that they needed to acquire enough money for two-year sailboat trips, while also needing to ensure employment upon returning from these extended vacations. No one was told to use this information; participants thought it was simply additional context.

Galinsky and Maddux found that the people who had lived abroad the longest had the most successful negotiations; they reached deals where shared interests were included in the solutions. For example, sellers provided discounts below their supposed price limits in exchange for guarantees that they would receive jobs at the gas stations after returning from their sailing trips—which also satisfied the buyers' needs for managers to run those stations. This is an interesting finding in itself, but the research didn't stop there.

In another experiment with people who had lived abroad, Galinsky and Maddux asked their subjects to draw aliens. They found that people who had lived in another country and who were instructed to think about their experiences of adapting themselves to another culture immediately before drawing their aliens were much more creative than those who didn't think about their cross-cultural experiences. Their drawings were more interesting, unusual, and less stereotypical than the depictions from the other subjects.

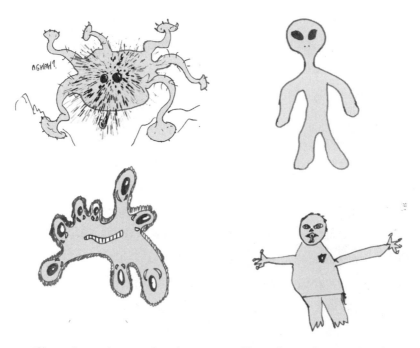

Aliens drawn by people who thought about cross-cultural experiences

Aliens drawn by people who didn't think about cross-cultural experiences

Examples from the Alien Drawing Experiment[38]

One way to better understand what could be going on with each of these studies is by taking a look at something most all of us know about: table manners. If you're from Japan, you know that making a slurping noise when drinking soup directly out of a bowl is perfectly acceptable, whereas in the United States that is considered pretty rude. If you're from Russia, you know it's polite to leave a little food on your plate at the end of the meal to signify that your host's hospitality was abundant and plentiful; in the United States, it's generally considered impolite not to finish what's on your plate. In India, people generally eat food using their right hands (because historically they do their "business" with their left), whereas in most other countries it doesn't matter which hand you use. These are just a few examples of cultural differences that become second nature based on where we live. And the list could go on regarding the various meanings and appropriateness of behavior for everything from public displays of affection, to how you greet business colleagues, to how you shop.

You may be wondering why I'm going on about table manners and aliens and gas stations (not to mention bus drivers who aren't really driving buses!). I'm not trying to say that people who have lived in different countries are somehow superior to those who have lived in only one place all their lives. What I'm trying to say is this: The more open we are to new experiences and different ways of being, the better. When we've lived in multiple cultures or at least exposed ourselves to a variety of cultural traditions, the notions of the "right way" versus the "wrong way" begin to break down; we recognize that there are alternative approaches; we see connections and patterns that we would never have seen otherwise. Our underlying mindsets shift in how we think about and approach problems and opportunities. In short, we lose rigidity. We grow more mentally limber. We find solutions that others might never imagine.

These conclusions are similar to what Galinsky and Maddux found across all their experiments: People who understand cultural differences see more options and possibilities when faced with tough challenges. Individuals who have spent extended periods of time living in different cultures are usually forced to reconcile conflicting values, norms, and behaviors. Their experience, in turn, leads them to be more flexible in their thinking, helps them make associations and connections between things that others don't see, and gives them a natural aptitude for looking at the underlying reasons why things work the way they do.

So, how does all this relate to leapfrogging? After we have listened to ourselves and obtained a general sense of our initial focus, the next phase involves taking proactive steps to both inform and challenge our mindsets. The goal is to experience new things that trigger us to toss out old beliefs, establish new assumptions, and gain insight into additional areas that we should further explore so that we can repeat this cycle of learning. The best way to do this is to go and explore—to talk to others outside our daily grind, immerse ourselves in others' lives, build relationships with unlikely people and partners, and do things that we wouldn't normally do.

During the first step of the leapfrogging process—Listen—we focused internally and listened to ourselves. Now it's time to look externally and explore.

Questions to Consider

⮞ Have you ever visited, lived, or worked in another country? What was your experience? What differences in values, norms, and behaviors did you notice? How were you affected?

⮞ When was the last time you experienced something that really challenged your assumptions? What happened?

New Insights Come from Pushing Beyond Comfort Zones

New insights and ideas rarely happen when we remain seated at our desks. That's why, as part of writing this book, I went out and spoke to many former clients and colleagues about their experiences with leapfrogging. One of these people was Steve Paljieg, Senior Director of Corporate Innovation at Kimberly-Clark. Steve's had a long career in marketing and product innovation, having held several senior roles at Procter & Gamble before assuming his current position.

When I asked Steve to tell me about the biggest single thing he's learned about innovation, he quickly responded with a simple one-liner: "Being open to surprises is something I've learned, and which I've learned to appreciate." Several years ago I worked with Steve and his team, and what happened during the project took us all by surprise and has since helped the entire organization move in an exciting new direction. Here's what happened and why it's a great example of what can occur when you push yourself beyond your comfort zone.

As the maker of Kleenex, Kotex, Depends, Huggies, and other products, Kimberly-Clark is already a leader in most of its markets. But they were looking for the next big thing, something they could develop into another hit. So they assembled a team to explore the options and asked me for assistance with guiding the process.

One of the first things we did was set up several innovation sessions to explore possible new directions. As a way to spur our creativity and push beyond our current mindsets, we invited a number of outsiders to the sessions—external experts in fields related to (and also unrelated to) Kimberly-Clark's core businesses. One of these leaders was Maria Bailey, a renowned author and talk show host, and the go-to authority on anything and everything related to motherhood. Steve was sharing a cup of coffee and chatting with Maria during a break between sessions when she brought up an interesting cultural phenomenon. All around the country, mothers themselves were inventing new child care products. "Why not reach out to these 'mompreneurs' and see what they're working on?" Maria asked. Steve was immediately intrigued by the idea. Going one step further, Steve thought, "Why not push beyond just seeing what innovative moms are doing by finding a way to innovate with them?"

"I realized that the only way to do it right was to go out directly to the innovators, to the moms themselves," Steve recalled. "These are the people who have the need and who have already translated it into solutions." Steve was definitely willing to work with these "mothers of invention." But he knew that it would be a radical departure from how Kimberly-Clark usually developed new products—and that the process would require some serious innovation in its own right to succeed.

The main question was how to do it, and the answer wasn't entirely clear. In fact, it led to even more questions, none of which was easy to answer either. For instance, how would he find these mompreneurs? Then, once he'd found them, how would he structure the company's financial and operating relationship with them? Would Kimberly-Clark simply offer to buy them out? Or could a more collaborative model be arranged?

Steve settled on a kind of hybrid approach. Instead of acquiring the rights to the inventions, Kimberly-Clark would provide sizable grants to fund the mompreneurs' own businesses. But this wouldn't be just a charity initiative. In exchange for the initial funding, Kimberly-Clark would get the right of first refusal if the moms ever decided to sell their stakes. Finally, instead of spending millions to find and evaluate these fledgling businesses, Steve realized that he could let the moms themselves come to him. He went back to the source of his original insight, Maria Bailey, and asked her to advertise the grant program to her millions of followers. Maria gladly agreed, and quality submissions immediately started pouring in.

The first dozen $15,000 "Huggies MomInspired Grants" were awarded to women with products as varied as a two-piece zippered bed sheet for cribs to a sippy cup that accelerates children's motor skills development. Since then, another round of grant applications has begun and Kimberly-Clark has even taken the program overseas, launching a similar MomInspired initiative in Australia.

All told, Kimberly-Clark funded the entire MomInspired program for a fraction of the cost of what they would have spent to create a prototype of any one of the dozen selected products. In return, the company not only has received massive amounts of positive (and free) media attention but also has built solid relationships with the grantees that could lead to profitable partnerships in the future. "The value of the program has been incredible," Steve said. "We've had over fifteen million web page views and social media references that promote our program and our brand. And the best thing is, it's not us driving it. It's the moms themselves. They are the new ambassadors for Huggies. You just can't buy PR like that."

The process behind Huggies MomInspired has helped the company see and do things differently. Steve summed this up when he said, "I think it's a little too proud to believe that our knowledge is perfect. We didn't go into that session looking for alternative business models to source innovation. But then again, that's the beauty of how these things work sometimes." Today the organization recognizes the value of surprises and how going *outside* one's comfort zone can help challenge and advance mindsets *inside*.

For Steve, all of this is indeed rewarding to see, but there's a deeper dynamic and greater intent underneath the visible business results. "It's been such an emotionally rich journey for me," Steve reflected. "I mean, moms will say to me that 'until I got this grant, I couldn't decide whether to keep my kid's college fund or start my business. You have solved this problem for me.'"

And that emotional richness ran even deeper than Steve initially realized. His mother passed away just before the first MomInspired grants were awarded. At a young age, she had worked at a neighborhood family grocery store. When she was sixteen, the owners decided to close the store and retire, but they gave her the unique opportunity to take it over, which she did. Steve's mother ran that little business for more than three decades. But it wasn't until Steve was writing her eulogy that he consciously realized the connection between his mother's experience and the program he'd just worked so hard to bring to life. "My mom was a great example of a woman who, against all odds, was able to build a successful business and provide for another generation of her family. I really think of MomInspired as payback for all that she was able to do and all the sacrifices she made."

Questions to Consider

- ➲ When have you done something that really pushed you outside your comfort zone? What happened?

- ➲ What new insights did you gain that either challenged your assumptions or led to new ideas?

Empathy Leads to Surprise

The late photojournalist Dan Eldon once asked, "What is the difference between exploring and being lost?" When it comes down to it, there's only a subtle distinction—which was exactly Dan's point. Feeling lost and feeling like we're exploring are both a state of mind. Gaining clarity into our next breakthrough involves going down paths that may take us nowhere or that may indeed lead us in promising new directions. When we explore new avenues and possibilities, we must tolerate feeling lost, since it's often a necessary part of the journey toward finding greater clarity.

The Explore phase of the leapfrogging process is about giving ourselves the types of experiences that can expand our awareness in the same ways that living in a different culture might naturally give us. But to do this, we can't be afraid to talk to people who are different from ourselves. We can't be fearful of putting ourselves into ambiguous and uncomfortable situations that literally force us to move outside of our comfort zones. The goal is to explore new things that move us from broad knowledge to targeted new insights about our breakthroughs. Here's how it often works:

- We go out and explore something that delivers new *knowledge*—experiences that provide context and information about something we didn't know before.

- By doing this, we gain a deeper *understanding* of the domain of our breakthrough—the issues, challenges, connections, and relationships that exist within the area.

- With this understanding, we then develop a sense of *empathy* for those involved—a deeper feeling for how people are affected by their current situations as well as a sense of their hopes for the future.

- With this empathy comes *insight*—further clarity about how we can make a big difference and why what we could do will matter to other people as well as to ourselves.

- The cycle repeats as we use our new insight to fuel the focus of our next exploration.

Here's another story that brings the dynamics of this "cycle of experiential exploration" to life: In 2004, senior leadership at Philips knew they had to make drastic changes. Over the preceding three years, the Dutch electronics company had lost billions of dollars

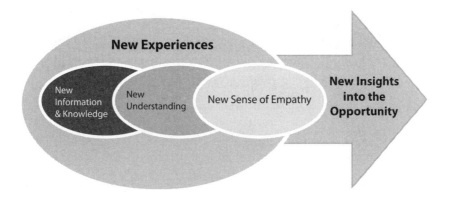

New Experiences

New Information & Knowledge

New Understanding

New Sense of Empathy

New Insights into the Opportunity

Experiential Exploration

due to stiff competition and falling prices in their core businesses of computer chips, compact-disc players, and televisions. Things were getting urgent.

Even in the midst of its financial crisis, Philips' leadership managed to find clarity. They knew they needed to get into a whole new business area, one that would draw upon their strengths as an organization. And they saw their U.S.-based medical systems unit, which provided X-rays, CAT scanners, and fetal monitors to hospitals, as the starting point. The idea was to somehow combine health care with consumer products to address a growing worldwide challenge—how to help the elderly live independently for as long as possible. If Philips could make just a small dent in this problem, they could save hospitals and governments millions, improve the lives of the elderly, and dig themselves out of their financial hole all at the same time. But a gigantic question remained: What specifically should they do?

Enter Jeannette de Noord, a twenty-year company veteran with a unique sense of Dutch practicality infused with a creative Silicon Valley–type mindset. Jeannette headed up a team with members from The Netherlands and the United States to research the elder care market and decide on the best way for Philips to get involved. I was brought in to help facilitate the process. Jeannette and I quickly decided that finding the right direction was going to take a little bit of blind orienteering, so to speak. We'd have to strike out into new areas—and maybe even get a little lost along the way.

One of the most powerful experiences came when we took the team on a visit to Sun City, Arizona. Sun City is the first community in the United States specifically planned and designed for retirees. There's a minimum age residency requirement of fifty-five to live there. Most organizations and city services in Sun City are run and operated by residents. The city's traffic cops, coffee shop, grocery store, and bowling alley employees are all seniors. The staffs in all seven of the city's recreation centers are seniors. Everywhere you look, you see gray hair.

The team spent two days with several Sun City residents who served as our guides. We spoke to the directors of the city's social services organizations. We visited people in their apartments and homes. We toured the various volunteer clubs. We went lawn bowling. We rode in golf carts. We ate at local restaurants and dined in cafeterias located within assisted living facilities. And we had the pleasure of getting to know people there.

One day, we chatted with a sprightly ninety-year-old woman who insisted to us that she wasn't old. When we asked her to clarify what she meant, she said, "My neighbor is 100. Now, *that's* old!" Almost everyone we spoke to in Sun City had a similar outlook. They defined "old" as anyone who had lived ten or fifteen years longer than they had. It didn't matter if they were seventy or ninety, they said the same thing. Another person, a man in his eighties, spoke to us about his philosophy on life. He said, "Being old is an attitude."

Within a few months, the team had gathered all the statistics, facts, and figures on the elderly we could ever want. But talking to the folks in Sun City helped us use that knowledge to gain a deeper understanding. We realized that we could all personally relate to the people we had met, as well as their experiences of growing older but still feeling young. My great grandmother, for example, had taught herself to paint when she was in her eighties, and although she died at 101 a few years ago, my family still enjoys her inspirational art in our homes today. Other members of the team had cared for their parents, grandparents, or other relatives at one time or another due to injuries or illnesses. And all of us realized that we ourselves would one day go through a similar process. Now, all of a sudden, we weren't just talking about some abstract population or target demographic. We were talking about real live people—our fellow human beings. Our knowledge had evolved into understanding, which had turned into something much richer and more valuable: empathy.

When we started the project, we all thought of the elderly as "old"—people who are different from the rest of the society. What we came to see was that the elderly are simply . . . people. They have the same needs as everyone else. They may have physical challenges that come and go, but at the deepest level, they're really no different than anyone else. When we stopped thinking of seniors as a target market to "care for" and instead as people who want to stay connected to their loved ones, remain living in their homes for as long as possible, have stylish things that are cool, continue to have joyous experiences, and contribute to society as productive citizens, things changed for everyone on the team.

Jeannette became the master at connecting this newfound perspective to insights about what Philips could do. She saw that the vast majority of existing products and services in the elder care market sacrificed dignity by telegraphing the messages "I'm old," "I'm incapable," and "I'm dependent." We realized the team needed to find solutions that hit the sweet spot among three things that really matter to people as they age: preserving self-reliance; staying connected to friends, family members, and the community; and overcoming the challenges of physical decline.

Once we settled on these three key ingredients, dozens of ideas surfaced. Because Philips had to move quickly, the decision was made to get into the market in a bigger and faster way than they could if they developed products from scratch. Over the next two years, Philips purchased Lifeline and Health Watch, two of the leading companies in the field of "at-home personal monitoring and emergency response services." These services give people a stylishly designed watch, pendant, or phone with a direct line to an operator who can communicate with them anytime, 24/7, for small things or major emergencies. A press release announcing the acquisition of Health Watch described the connection between the team's insights and Philips' new business by noting that the service "gives independently-minded seniors the confidence to maintain an active life at home."[39] This peace of mind extends to the seniors' families as well, who are often paying the monthly fees.

These acquisitions propelled Philips into the consumer healthcare market and instantly created entirely new revenue streams through recurring services fees for the company. It wasn't long before Jeannette's project was heralded by *The Wall Street Journal* as helping to turn the company around.[40] Today, Philips' Lifeline serves almost one million seniors and their families every minute of the day and night.

As I look back on this project, I still feel a great connection to the many people I met during our work. The experience affected all of us. We gained knowledge of a new market and achieved an intellectual understanding of the ins and outs of the lives of seniors. This understanding helped us develop a deeper empathy for other people, which led us to insights about what we could provide that would make a real difference to these seniors and their families.

We don't necessarily have to travel around the world to find these kinds of insights. Sometimes it's just a matter of visiting a neighborhood we normally don't venture into, talking to new people, or eating foods we don't normally eat. What's important is that we push outside of our comfort zones to discover new things that help us see the world, other people, and ourselves in new ways. When we give empathy to others, we often get something surprising in return.

Questions to Consider

- ➲ Think about a time where you felt "lost" but came out on the other side more knowledgeable or insightful. What happened and why?

- ➲ Have you ever had a conversation with someone that resulted in empathy for that person or another group? What happened? How did this change your mindset or affect you?

Making It Real

We talked about the fact that you can't see your assumptions and mindsets until you've already bypassed them. We looked at research that shows how flexible thinking, creative problem solving, and finding opportunities are tied to one's mindsets and assumptions, and how it's important to push beyond our comfort zones in ways that reinforce these qualities. And we discussed how Kimberly-Clark and

Philips explored new areas in ways that generated a sense of empathy for others, which in turn led to surprising insights that fueled new business opportunities.

The goal of the second step in the leapfrogging process is to get up, get out, and begin exploring new things to initiate the process of breaking down our limiting assumptions and mindsets. This is often achieved by using the clarity we already possess to structure what and how we go about immersing ourselves in the possibilities. Here are some activities to help make all this real. Conduct these in sequence or pick and choose depending on your needs.

 ## Leapfrogging Tools

1. Get Surprised by Past Surprises

Make a list of the surprises you've seen in your industry. Look at how each of these breakthroughs overcame various assumptions and barriers. Consider what these examples tell you about what's limiting thinking, constraining possibilities, or boxing you into current mindsets. Look at how what you learn has implications for how you might bypass today's mindsets to create new opportunities.

Consider the following questions as you do this:

- Who created these surprises? Did they come from inside or outside your industry? What gave them their unique ability to conceive of and create the breakthrough when no one else had done something similar before?

- What mindsets did these innovators possess that differed from how other people were seeing the world at the time?

- How did these breakthroughs influence the mindsets of other people?

- What are similar assumptions and mindsets that may be limiting your thinking today?

2. Intrigue Yourself

Getting clear on what you really want to know and learn is a critical first step in figuring out what to explore. Create a list of your "areas of intrigue"—the things you really want to learn more about. These may be topics that will help you to fill in gaps in your knowledge, or they may be things you'd like to simply better understand about various subjects.

- List up to a dozen areas of intrigue. Examples might be *board games children like most*, *the healthiest yet best tasting desserts*, and *the most successful Twitter users*.

- For each topic, create a list of guiding questions that, if answered, would really give you a solid understanding of the area. For instance, using the example of *board games children like most*, you could come up with questions like: What are the most popular children's board games? How long do the best games take to play? Do adults usually play with the children? What does it take to win?

This exercise will help you better understand what's most important to explore—although it's usually best to prioritize and select your top three to five areas to start in order to keep things manageable. Once you've got your focus, you can go on to the next step and venture out to get some empathy.

3. Get Some Empathy

Empathy is about stepping into another person's shoes, to see and feel things from another's perspective. It's possible to experience empathy from watching a great movie, reading an engaging book, or listening to compelling stories. If you've ever watched a moving film and gotten choked up, you know what I mean. But the most powerful and useful method for leapfrogging is to immerse ourselves directly in others' lives. This can be done in a number of different ways—from moving to another country (at one extreme) to simply talking to someone with an inquisitive, open mind. Each of us possesses a different natural capacity for empathy, but there are also tools and techniques to assist us in the process. Here are some things you can do:

- Go out and talk to people. Find individuals, groups, or organizations who you think can address your most important questions, either directly by answering them or indirectly through describing their daily lives, hopes, desires, dreams, problems, or challenges. These can be "experts" or they can simply be regular "laypeople." Talk to them on the phone or meet with them. Get to know them by interviewing them, rolling up your sleeves with them where they work or play, or doing whatever makes sense based on what you want to learn and experience. You may need to do a little digging or networking to find or get access to these people, but through Facebook, LinkedIn, or other resources, getting out there is easier than ever before.

- Go out and observe people. Find places and venues that relate to your areas of intrigue and related questions. Put yourself in a different physical environment by going to organizations, neighborhoods, cultural events, social or sporting events, and other places that you wouldn't normally visit.

- A lot of work has been done on using empathy to inform and inspire the design of new products. Check out the Stanford Design School's "Bootcamp Bootleg" manual, a guide that provides simple and practical tools for the entire innovation process, including the first step they call *Empathize*. The manual provides tools for shifting your mindset, interviewing people, and engaging in other practical activities. Just do a web search for "Stanford Design School Bootleg" and you're sure to find it. It's good stuff.

- Empathy comes from internalizing what it feels like to be in others' shoes—it involves vicariously experiencing emotions, which can range from joy to pain. As you talk to or observe people, consider the following questions:

  - What gives them a sense of purpose?
  - What is most important to them?
  - What are their concerns?
  - What are their biggest problems or challenges?
  - How do their circumstances, business context, or life context influence their mindsets, attitudes, and behaviors?

4. Expand Your Boundaries

Our mindsets limit our ability to consider alternatives and possibilities that go beyond the boundaries of our assumptions. Our boundaries are shaped by our beliefs about what's possible, feasible, or valued. They can be about personal skills, team knowledge and abilities, organizational capabilities, market needs, technology, business charters, financial requirements, partnership possibilities, competition, and just about anything else. Here are a few things you can do that go beyond the usual brainstorming to help expand your boundaries in ways that can lead to bigger breakthroughs:

- *Adapt a "Business Model."* Find a company completely outside of your industry or market and look at what makes it different and what it does really well. Then adapt the model to your cause. John Mullins and Randy Komisar,[41] authors of *Getting to Plan B*, offer a simple approach to expanding one's perspective. Just complete the following sentence:

  "I want to be the _____ of _____"
  by putting a company name in the first blank and the area of your breakthrough in the second blank. For example, if you want to transform the fashion industry, you might try "I want to be the Netflix of fashion," which could lead you down the path toward high-end evening gown rental services. Consider the following companies, or add your own ideas to the list:

Starbucks	NIKE
Netflix	Home Depot
ING Bank	Google
Twitter	Microsoft
Groupon	Coca-Cola
Burberry	American Automobile Association (AAA)
Ebay	American Association of Retired Persons (AARP)
Amazon	
Domino's Pizza	The Red Cross
Apple	The World Bank

■ *Ponder Improbable Partnerships.* Similar to the business model activity, consider potential partnerships with companies far outside your industry. Think about "what if" scenarios, such as What if we partnered with Coca-Cola or FedEx or Disney? The goal isn't necessarily to find a partnership, but rather to use the unusual pairing to stimulate thinking that pushes beyond boundaries. Go down the list of companies listed before or add your own. Consider these questions:

◻ What would the partnership allow you to do that you can't do today?

◻ What assumptions would the partnership challenge in your existing industry?

◻ How can you take some of the most interesting aspects of this partnership and weave them into your breakthrough?

6

Act:
Take Small Simple Steps,
Again and Again and Again

All great things have small beginnings.

—Peter Senge

Chapter Six Key Messages

1. Large leaps begin with small steps.

2. Small steps start big cycles of learning.

3. The best first steps are sophisticatedly simple.

4. Surprises provide clues about what to do next.

Over the last decade, Apple has been consistently ranked as one the most innovative companies in the world by the vast majority of trade groups and publications. So let me ask: How many times have you heard about Apple's intention of transforming the music industry with its iPods and iTunes? Probably lots. And it makes sense—they've done something that's truly transformative.

In fact, Steve Jobs was once quoted in an interview as saying, "When we created the iTunes Music Store, we did that because we thought it would be great to be able to buy music electronically, not because we had plans to redefine the music industry."[42] Looking back, it's probably not too strong of a statement to say that Apple actually *disrupted* the music industry with iTunes. But did Apple know it was doing this at the time? No! Apple created iTunes because it felt like the right thing to do at the time. It was a solitary step that had unintended—yet quite positive (at least for Apple)—consequences.

Peter Sims, author of *Little Bets*, says that "entrepreneurs don't begin with brilliant ideas—they discover them,"[43] something he saw over and over again as a venture capitalist in Silicon Valley. Sims's book title is his core premise: that most breakthrough ideas emerge over time from "little bets" that give us ways to reduce risk by starting small and using trial and error to refine and build out our ideas.

One of Sims's examples is Google, which first came onto the scene as a simple search box in the middle of a blank white computer screen. Larry Page and Sergey Brin didn't start the company with the intention of transforming the Internet, buying YouTube, or launching the Android operating system on smartphones and tablet computers. Their very first step—and what kicked off their journey—was to find a more effective and robust way to prioritize library searches online (yes, *library* searches!). From there, they realized they could also prioritize general Internet web pages. But, even after they achieved this feat, they still didn't have a recipe for making money. It wasn't until they created Adwords, which allowed them to tie online advertising to the specific searches that people made, that things really took off. From there, one thing led to the next, and that little search box turned into a whole lot more.

This chapter's core concept is simple: *By taking a series of small steps, we begin a cycle of learning that leads to bigger and greater things.* Through simplifying our ideas and using trial and error, we

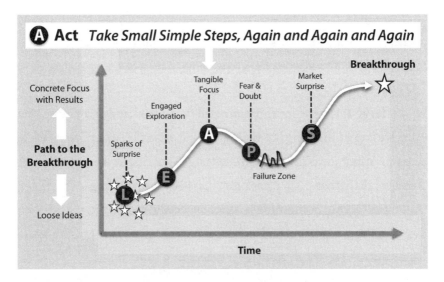

Act Phase of the Leapfrogging Life Cycle

can test and push our thinking. As we do this, we learn more about our challenges, our opportunities, and ourselves, which allows us to bypass our limiting mindsets and move closer to achieving our breakthroughs.

Small Steps Can Lead to Big Things

Four Seasons is a great story of how small steps produced a big leap. Barbara Talbott's success at Four Seasons started with two small steps: moving high-end photos onto the website and listing a new 800 number. Taking these steps allowed her team to get going during a time of great uncertainty and ambiguity. It wasn't always a smooth ride, however. At one point, Barbara and her team segmented their website into different "travel experiences"—with separate portals for things like business travel, vacations, and conferences. After launching the new design, everyone realized it was much too cumbersome, so they threw it out and started over. Call this a failure or call it trial and error, either way, this bump in the road allowed Barbara's team to learn more about what *didn't* work so that they could move on to find what *did*.

The goal is to become comfortable with trial and error. Opening ourselves up to the fact that we may be surprised by what comes back, that our initial ideas and hypotheses might have been wrong, helps set the stage. Whether it's a pleasant surprise or a surprising setback, the process of giving something a shot, succeeding or failing, and then ascertaining what happened is a surefire way to move things forward. Here's another research study that delves into this further.

Two business school researchers, Saras Sarasvathy and Stuart Read, set out to better understand the unique behaviors of people who are known for diving into things, so they studied the mindsets of serial entrepreneurs.[44] Sarasvathy looked for the cream of the crop—entrepreneurs who had at least fifteen years of experience, had started multiple companies (both successes and failures), and had taken at least one company public during their careers. Meanwhile, Read looked to contrast the entrepreneurs with professional managers from a variety of large corporations, including leaders from Shell, Philip Morris, and Nestlé. In each case, people were given the same hypothetical case study of a start-up company and asked to respond to various questions and issues that the CEO would need to address to build and grow the firm. Sarasvathy and Read spent two hours with each of their subjects, recording everything they said. Using their mountain of data, they analyzed and compared the thinking and problem-solving styles of both groups.

The entrepreneurs didn't start out by listing concrete goals. Instead, they looked at the resources and information they had to work with, figured out their short-term actions, and then improvised with a give-and-take mindset. They didn't care about detailed planning and analysis; their primary objective was to get something tangible out into the hands of customers, even if it wasn't fully baked. All of their initial effort was focused on doing something as real as possible and then quickly learning more about what was needed, what worked and what didn't. Most important, they didn't assume that they had the right answers to these questions. In fact, they'd modify their ideas using input from just about anyone—advisors, suppliers, customers, and others—something even the most humble of us have a hard time doing. Sarasvathy says her findings suggest that entrepreneurs don't believe they can predict the future, so they don't try. Rather, they try to create it for themselves, one step at a time.

The professional managers, on the other hand, worked in very different ways. They established specific goals and then created detailed plans to achieve them. They saw data—like customer research and competitive analyses—as a critical requirement before they could take action. They viewed customer relationships as take and give, with the underlying objective of *taking* detailed information from customers in order to *give* them a final product or service to meet their stated needs. Sarasvathy attributed this radically different approach to a mindset that believes the future—or at least elements of it—can be predicted and that the job of the manager is to create plans that control how things will unfold. In other words, entrepreneurs look for surprises, while professional managers avoid them.

So, what does this tell us about leapfrogging? Creating breakthroughs is indeed more skewed toward the entrepreneurial mindset. This isn't to say that if you're part of a large organization it's going to be impossible to leapfrog; we've already looked at some great examples that came from big companies. But, speaking from experience working within a corporation that has more than 120,000 employees, I know that these kinds of organizations tend to value the virtues of predictability and certainty. In other words, they reinforce the managerial mindset, which is diametrically opposed to the idea of surprise. And, while many managers in large companies approach things one step at a time, their steps are often tied to predefined goals. If a step in the plan—or the goal itself—isn't achieved because of a surprising development, it's seen (and treated) as a failure rather than an opportunity to change the course of action or create a new, more relevant and better goal.

When it comes to breakthroughs, every step is a learning opportunity. Trying to predict or control the future constrains our mindsets, which is why small steps that allow us remain flexible are essential to the process. By intentionally taking small steps, we're able to test assumptions through feet-on-the-ground actions, so we can quickly validate them or throw them out and start over. Sometimes we simply validate our hypotheses, while other times we may experience a real surprise that suggests a radical redirection.

Questions to Consider

➲ When have you seen a small idea morph and transform into something much larger? What happened and why?

➲ When have you, your team, or your organization demonstrated the characteristics of the entrepreneurs in the research study? What happened?

➲ What characteristics of entrepreneurs come easiest to you? Which are much less natural for you? Why do you think this is?

The Best Steps Are Sophisticatedly Simple

Leonardo da Vinci once said "simplicity is the ultimate sophistication." When it comes to leapfrogging, simplicity is indeed the most sophisticated solution for moving an idea from concept to reality. The reason: One of the keys to being able to "act" is to simplify.

When we're bogged down in details, complexity, and overwhelming options, it often becomes hard to move. Simplification can help get us going again; it is all about boiling down complexity to its core essence. The ironic thing is that making something simple can be really, really hard. For example, rather than writing a twenty-page business plan, it can actually be more effective to make it a single page—but creating this one-pager might actually be twenty times harder than writing the treatise on how we're planning to change the world. That's because, to simplify something, we have to understand its most vital elements, its guts and bones. And we have to be able to clearly articulate these key points and explain why what we're doing really matters.

Sometimes our small steps can involve going out into the world to explore it in a general way, as in the example of the Philips team from the preceding chapter. But small steps can also be much more action-oriented and involve doing something that is as tangible as possible, and then seeing what happens. Many in the product development world already do this in the form of rapid prototyping—making a product or service, getting it out there, and learning from how people respond to it. Google is the master of this approach, which they communicate to the world by including the word *beta* next to many of their product logos. Gmail, for example, was considered an experiment and had *beta* next to it for five years—yes, *five* years!

Remember Steve Paljieg and his Huggies MomInspired project? It's a perfect example of how simplification can jump-start a breakthrough. From the beginning, Steve's goal wasn't to "sell" some grand vision to others, but rather to create a discussion around his basic idea for the program. The only thing Steve ever used to push his plan was a one-page write-up. "Most people can't have a conversation without a 30 page PowerPoint, but that's just not my style," Steve proclaimed. "If I can't present a compelling case on one piece of paper, then there's no way I can expect anyone else to understand what I'm doing."

People responded to Steve's one-pager with a lot more than their own ideas. They also reacted with enthusiasm and support because Steve's openness allowed them to assume a sense of ownership in the project as well. Like the serial entrepreneurs in Sarasvathy and Read's study, Steve used these new partners and their input to strengthen his original idea—and also to update his one-page overview. Indeed, he told me that the core idea behind Huggies MomInspired morphed in various ways for the better over time. His eagerness to take input, change his assumptions, and adapt the concept based on things he learned from others during his "one-page dialogues" eventually resulted in his final product: a dynamic new program that has benefited the company in big ways. But that big breakthrough would have never happened without a whole bunch of small simple steps followed by adjustments and recalibrations along the way.

Questions to Consider

➲ Can you describe the core essence of your idea in no more than two sentences?

➲ What's *not* critically important about your idea?

➲ What is the smallest, simplest step you could take that would have the greatest impact?

Surprises Provide Clues about What to Do Next

In Greek mythology, the oracle at Delphi was famous for giving tricky answers when people asked about the future. She once told a famous king that if he invaded Persia, "a mighty empire would fall." Of course, she neglected to name which empire she was talking about (it turned out to be the king's own). In other words, there was a lot of wiggle room in the oracle's prognostications. It was all about interpretation and, most important, adapting plans accordingly.

When we get surprised, our surprises can tell us important things. We've already talked about how surprises signal things about our assumptions, like when we eat Pop Rocks we might think "I didn't know a candy could do that!" But surprises can also act like the oracle at Delphi—they can provide powerful clues about what to do next.

One of the reasons for starting with small, simple steps is so that we can test out our assumptions and learn about them without too much exposure to the downside. When we're going for breakthroughs, we're usually exploring uncharted territory, so we're learning new things all the time. Paying attention to our bigger surprises—the things that really give us a jolt—can signal whether we're on the right track or we need to shift our mindsets and do things differently. I call these "pop-up guideposts," since they pop up unexpectedly in the middle of a journey and keep us moving in the right direction.

Barbara Talbott's two big pop-up guideposts at Four Seasons were the Wall Street analyst's report and the fact that more customers were looking for vacations on the website. Both helped Barbara conclude that there was a bigger strategic business opportunity in repositioning Four Seasons as a global hotel and resort brand. They also gave her team their next steps—namely, to further build out their website with a global vacation focus.

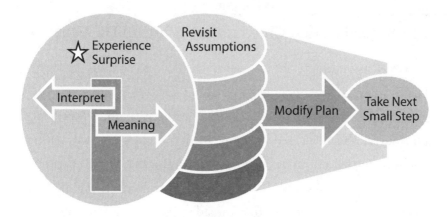

Dynamics of Pop-up Guideposts

It's somewhat ironic to describe these pop-up guideposts as surprises because they are one of the more predictable things that happen when leapfrogging. When we put ourselves out there with the intention of testing our ideas and assumptions, it's only natural that we'll be surprised by what comes back. If we don't find some unexpected results, we're probably exploring something that's fairly mundane—and most likely pretty well short of turning into a breakthrough.

Remember David Levin, founder of the KIPP Academies from Chapter One? Needless to say, an affluent guy from the suburbs experienced a whole host of jolting surprises when he started his first charter middle school in inner-city Houston. One of his most important discoveries came from a surprising situation that threatened to derail his experiment almost as soon as it had begun. Early on, the district added seventeen new kids to the eleven he had started with. Levin put them in groups facing each other in order to symbolize that his teaching approach would be very different from the traditional classroom model. But there was a problem, a big one. "What no one had told me," he recalls, "is that they were from rival gangs."

Clearly, this could have been a major disaster, and in fact there were bets—a running pool with odds—on whether Levin would make it past Thanksgiving. But this watershed moment turned into a pop-up guidepost for Levin and helped direct him toward a real breakthrough. He realized that he needed to replace the kids' loyalty to gangs with loyalty to one another and to the school. To accomplish this, he had the students perform special group chants and songs, like you might find at a summer camp. The experiment worked. The new classmates bonded and started seeing themselves as KIPP students first and gang members second. Today, KIPP schools are known for these incredibly effective songs and chants. But the practice wasn't born in some theoretical vision statement or business plan. It came from a real-world moment of crisis, a critical sink-or-swim juncture early in the organization's history.

Speaking of school, here's a story about an innovator I've known since we attended high school together. Even back then, Chuck Templeton was the kind of guy who was always pushing the limits. I don't know whether he would have made it in the highly structured environment of a KIPP academy. It's hard to say how many times we drove past the school parking lot in the morning and headed to the beach instead. Chuck enjoyed a good time. He was also very, let's say, creative when it came to handling authority. He once jammed our school's door locks so we didn't have to take a test during first period.

Back in 1998, Chuck showed me a business plan for a new company he was starting called "EasyEats.com." He came up with the idea for this new venture after watching his wife struggle to make last-minute restaurant reservations for a weekend visit from her family. "She would call one place and get a reservation for Saturday, then she'd call another for Sunday and they'd be full so she'd have to switch the first one," he recalled to me recently by phone. "It went on for three hours and I just thought there had to be a better way to do this."

Chuck estimated that there were roughly 100 thousand restaurants in the United States hoping for customers to make reservations. Meanwhile, on any given night, there were some 30 million would-be diners looking for a good meal. So he set out to help both parties achieve their goals. The idea was that diners would log on to the EasyEats website and make reservations and, voila, the restaurants would fill their tables without having to lift a finger.

This core business model—using the Internet to put diners into available seats at restaurants—has remained constant over the past fourteen years, something pretty rare in the fast-paced technology world. But that's been the only constant. Just about everything else has changed.

First off, there was the name. Early on, Chuck discovered that upscale restaurants didn't particularly care to have their gourmet fare called "eats." So he and his team switched to the more refined-sounding "OpenTable." But Chuck then realized that the name change also meant he needed to recalibrate the company's goals. Initially, he had pitched EasyEats.com to investors as a precursor to a whole series of "Easy" online booking portals, like EasyCuts.com for hairstylist appointments and EasyPutts.com for golf reservations. Chuck came to realize that if the name of his company was being challenged by customers within a month of starting the company, one thing was clear: The opportunity lay in a tighter focus. So he ditched the broader plan and brought what he called a "maniacal focus" to changing the restaurant world.

Implementing the online reservation system was also much more challenging than Chuck expected. He originally assumed that restaurants would plug their existing reservation systems into an Internet connection and make their available seats accessible to the OpenTable.com website. But, after receiving several blank stares from local restaurant managers, he quickly learned that most restaurants weren't wired for the web yet. Even if they were, their computers were in the back office and the digital reservation systems he hoped to plug into didn't exist—the "systems" the restaurants used were in the form of a pad of paper at the receptionist stand.

To make his idea work, Chuck and his team had to tweak their approach once again. Instead of simply building and promoting a website primarily geared toward diners, the company had to cater much more to the restaurant side of the equation. To do this, Chuck found himself going into the computer hardware business. OpenTable began to install Electronic Reservation Books (ERBs) inside restaurants that used their service—essentially a computer with special reservation software at the receptionist desk. This extra infrastructure was initially a huge source of anxiety and pushback from investors. No one wanted the overhead, installation hassle, and support implications of dealing with all that wiring and equipment. But Chuck pushed on because he realized it was the only way to get any real traction for his business. "It got to the point that if the sales team could get a contract, we would do whatever was needed to get the system into the restaurant, from ordering their DSL to running the cables in the ceiling," Chuck told me. Interestingly enough, when you fast-forward to today, Chuck says these ERBs have actually become one of the company's core strengths. "Back in the day, everyone hated the fact that we were installing this ERB computer thing that we had to bring down to restaurants on the back of a moped," he recalled. "But now that's really what the market loves because it's like a protective moat around the business." Once a restaurant has a system, the switching costs are high. Chuck admits this wasn't originally by design, but when you consider that restaurants might have several years of data in the system, the next several weeks of reservations lined up in it, a staff that's been trained on how to use it, and a large percentage of their reservations coming through it, they're essentially locked in.

Open Table's new restaurant-centric focus coincided with a final shift, or "pivot-point" as Chuck describes it, in his mindset. Originally, he assumed that restaurants would be thrilled to subscribe to the OpenTable network because it would help them fill their tables. Who wouldn't want a full house every night? But in a meeting with New York restaurateur Danny Meyer, Chuck got yet another reality check. "Danny's got numerous restaurants in New York. He's an icon. And he really jolted us. He said, 'Look, I don't need more business. We're full every night.'" In that moment, Chuck realized that his prime target customer in one of the most important food cities in the country didn't need his service. "But as Danny went on he said, 'What I do need to know more about is the customers I already have, and how I can make their experience even more perfect.' I realized right there, 'Wow. We can do that, too!'"

Today OpenTable isn't a mere booking system for restaurants; it's a customer relationship and service enhancement tool. If a diner prefers a certain table or a special meal, OpenTable can help the manager or maitre'd make sure that she gets it. If a customer wants to surprise her spouse with an embarrassing birthday song over dessert, she just notes it down when making a reservation. Indeed, since that fateful meeting with Danny Meyer, the ease of making an online reservation for diners has turned into a relatively small facet of OpenTable's business. Helping restaurants ensure that those diners have the best possible experience has truly become the company's (ahem) bread and butter.

Again, Chuck's original idea for using the Internet—and now mobile devices—to bring networks of diners and restaurants together hasn't changed at all. But OpenTable might look very different from how it looks today if Chuck hadn't been so flexible in viewing his continual stream of surprises as guideposts to help direct the company's strategies and actions.

Sometimes pop-up guideposts are blindingly obvious and it's clear how to respond to them. Other times, their meanings might be a little bit more opaque, like the predictions of the oracle at Delphi. In those cases, it's all about interpretation and adaptation. . Whatever the case, it's critical to stay open-minded and to view surprises as opportunities that can help guide your next steps. Think about David Levin standing in front of a class full of rival gang members. He could have given up. He could have called the whole thing a failure. (A lot of people might have literally run for their lives at that point.) But, instead, he found the inspiration to remake the environment of the class and, in the process, he's now changed the lives of thousands of kids for the better.

Questions to Consider

➲ In your organization, do people talk about their surprises? If so, how do they use them? If not, what do you think is holding them back?

➲ When have you taken a small step and been surprised by the result? What happened, and what surprised you about it?

➲ Have you ever been surprised by something and as a result seen a pop-up guidepost? What happened?

Making It Real

We discussed how simplifying our ideas can help us take small steps that become the catalyst for cycles of learning and sometimes surprise. We looked at research that compared entrepreneurs and corporate managers, and we saw that most organizations are structured to avoid unexpected events while most entrepreneurs seek out inputs that challenge their assumptions as a key strategy for accelerating their learning. We saw how simplifying ideas can help us formulate our initial small steps. And we explored the ways in which surprises hold clues, or pop-up guideposts, about how to proceed during times of great uncertainty.

The goal of the third phase of the leapfrogging life cycle is to get out there and take small steps to get the ball rolling. By doing this, we're able to gain feedback and insight into our assumptions so we can quickly shift our mindsets and recalibrate our goals and actions to keep our breakthroughs moving forward.

 ## Leapfrogging Tools

1. Create Your One-Pager, Then Shop It Around

Steve Paljieg was successful at Kimberly-Clark because he had a compelling idea in Huggies MomInspired. But the idea wouldn't have gone anywhere if he hadn't been able to communicate it in a way that inspired even more great ideas from his colleagues. Steve described his approach as a slow process of gaining trust and sponsorship. "Every time I drew the circle a little bigger, people came in, got excited, and contributed to the thinking," he recalled. Creating a one-pager that tells your story can be a great small step that creates further clarity for yourself and allows others to react to your ideas. When they do react, they're essentially reacting to the assumptions and mindsets that went into creating the one-pager in the first place. Pay attention, since you never know when you'll encounter a valuable surprise. There's really no best format for the one-pager. The goal is to tell your story in your own way. But consider using text, graphics, art, or anything else that will captivate people. To get started, you might consider the following questions:

- In one or two sentences, what's the core of your idea?

- What do you hope your idea ultimately delivers for you, your organization, and the broader community and world?

- Whom will it benefit, and in what ways? Why will they care?

- What makes your idea uniquely different from existing ways of doing something or other ideas that are already out there?

- Where's the breakthrough? In what ways does the idea challenge the status quo?

- What key assumptions exist today that you hope to turn upside down?

- How will it all work?

- What assumptions do you *know* you're making?

- What are the things you still need to learn?

- What do you need to do to get started?

2. Cook Up a Small-Step Strategy

The great thing about small steps is that they're inherently less risky than big ones. Early on, the goal is to figure out the smallest steps that could have the biggest impact without overly committing to a single direction in order to leave options open. Ideally you want to go out there with something as tangible as possible. Sometimes it may be just your one-pager. But you can also get out there with drawings, prototypes, mock-ups, diagrams, or anything else that conveys your concept. Don't worry about developing a highly detailed "strategic plan" at this point. Just try to apply the direction you already have to what you can do to get out there and start making things happen. To help determine what your small steps should be, consider the following:

- What resources (technologies, knowledge, people, tools, relationships, etc.) do you have at your disposal right now?

- What other resources can you gain easy access to through your networks?

- How can you make your ideas as clear and as tangible as possible so others can instantly understand them—through prototypes, graphics, illustration, models, mock-ups, and so on?

- How might the framing of your concept need to differ depending on who you're sharing it with so they can see the implications for themselves in your ideas?

- Which potential customers will be open to hearing your ideas? What assumptions do you want to test with them, and what questions do you have for them?

- Which of your potential customers do you suspect will really hate your current thinking, and how can you get their input to strengthen your idea?

- How can you best engage customers, partners, suppliers, or others in an "informational interview" about your ideas, so they can provide input, get excited, and jump on board to support your efforts?

- What big things need to happen that you can tackle in small steps to start?

- What big things need to happen that you can put off for now?

- What is one small step that you can take right now?

3. Find Your Guideposts

Surprises happen all the time. The goal is to recognize them when they occur and to look for the ones that could make the most difference for your breakthroughs. When you go out and take action, tune into your surprises to explore what they say about what you should do next. When someone responds to your ideas, look for the following:

- Does their feedback and input make you cringe or put you at ease? When you cringe, what new ideas do you get that go beyond your current assumptions?

- Do you feel the desire to continue trying to convince them to accept your idea, or do you sense that they naturally "get it"?

- What does their response tell you about the match between what you care most about and what's most important to them?

- What does their response tell you about what's valid, incorrect, or debatable about your assumptions?

- What does their response tell you about their own assumptions and values? How can your ideas morph to incorporate what's most important to them?

- Given any issues, concerns, or areas of excitement that you have heard, what resources do you have or could you gain access to that can address them?

If you couldn't already tell, most of these questions are much more about *you* than about those giving you feedback. For example, if you recognize that you're squirming at what you're hearing, it likely means that your core assumptions are being challenged—which also means you'll probably need to recalibrate your direction. The goal is to use yourself as an "indicator" to help you determine which assumptions you hold that are useful guideposts and which may limit your opportunities.

7

Persist:
Take the Surprise
Out of Failure

Many of life's failures are people who did not realize
how close they were to success when they gave up.

—*Thomas Edison*

Chapter Seven Key Messages

1. You will fail.

2. External criticism comes from old assumptions.

3. Failure results from fear, not failure itself.

4. Reframing failures as stepping-stones keeps us going.

5. Optimism fuels action.

At many big companies, there's a lot of room for lip service but little room for real failure. We hear the catchphrases over and over: "We need to embrace failure," "Failure is necessary for success," "We must fail faster to succeed sooner," and so on. But as soon as the possibility of actual failure arises, suddenly all those comforting clichés go out the window. It's one thing to promote punchy phrases; it's another to live them.

Leapfrogging is about using failure as a tool to find success. Take Sarah Robb O'Hagan, President of Gatorade, for example. Having learned that many young football players pack bananas in their sport bags only to find them mashed between their cleats before practice, she asked her product development team to create a better alternative. The result: a pre-workout drink pouch containing a powerful carbohydrate punch. The ingredients weren't the challenge; it was the container. "We knew drink bottles like the backs of our hands, but pouches were a completely new animal," Sarah said.

Gatorade launched the pouch with lightning speed, hoping to make a big splash in the market by establishing a new product category. But, although the pouches had tested well in the lab setting, some of them leaked when sitting on store shelves—a pretty big problem for a product meant to be a cleaner alternative to mushy pre-workout snacks like bananas. In many organizations, customer complaints and internal grumblings would have stopped the entire program in its tracks. Rather than running for cover and placing blame, however, Sarah focused on personally managing the fallout while turning the problem into a learning opportunity.

Sarah helped her team "reframe failure" by using the experience to emphasize the importance of trial and error. "We could have waited another six months to 'get it right,'" she told me, "but we would have missed both the summer season and a great learning opportunity. In fact, the leaky pouches caused everyone to revisit their assumptions about the packaging, which led to an even better ergonomic design and superior packaging materials." As I'll describe in greater detail in the next chapter, the pre-workout drink pouch, along with several other products, ultimately became the foundation upon which Gatorade reinvented and re-energized its entire product line and brand.

A lot of big organizations like Gatorade know that fear of failure is a huge problem when it comes to fostering breakthroughs. Here are a few examples of what various companies do to help people overcome their fear of failure:

- Google gives its software engineers one day a week of free time to experiment with pet projects that everyone acknowledges may or may not yield benefits for the company. New products and software features often carry the label *beta* to indicate they're still a work in progress, so when problems arise, the expectation already exists that they won't be perfect right out of the gate.[45]

- The large Indian conglomerate Tata Group gives out an annual award for the "best failed idea." The goal is to recognize and reward failures, since without them, successes would be impossible.[46]

- Pharmaceutical company Eli Lilly hosts "failure parties" where employees come together to share their stories of failure and discuss what they learned from them.[47]

- In order to encourage risk taking, Facebook posts signs around the office that say things like "Done is better than perfect" and "What would you do if you weren't afraid?"

If any one of these practices was truly the silver bullet for creating business breakthroughs, every company would be doing it. While they may indeed help to create a climate where new ideas and experimentation are more encouraged, these practices really don't eliminate the underlying fear of failure associated with taking real risk or royally screwing up.

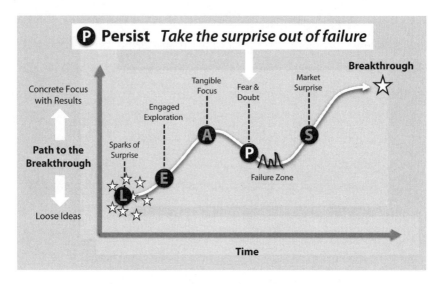

Persist Phase of the Leapfrogging Life Cycle

One of the biggest leadership challenges of our day is overcoming our deep-seated negative perception of failure. It's a big problem because here's a safe bet: When we're attempting to create something groundbreaking, we will experience failures along the way. Put a little more bluntly: You *will* fail. I know that's not the most motivating thing I could say to kick off this chapter, but it's true. When we're going for breakthrough success, we'll never get there by just relying on completely safe steps along the way. Like it or not, failure is an inherent part of the process. We need to be ready for it, willing to accept it, and able to respond to it in a productive way.

I'm not saying it's impossible to succeed without encountering difficulty or to flawlessly achieve our goals. But the fact is, it's pretty rare. The proverbial shit can happen, and often does. The deeper source of the problem of failure isn't necessarily the failure *itself* but rather the *fear* of failure before it even happens. Fear of failure keeps many people from taking a step into the unknown. Said another way, fear arises when we're scared—either consciously or unconsciously—of both negative surprises and negative scenarios that we've made up in our heads. And when we're afraid we'll fail, we can start doing some pretty unproductive things, including not even trying in the first place or giving up part way through the journey— and these things constitute *real* failure.

When we're doing something really big, feelings of uncertainty can overwhelm us. We can lose the sense of excitement and motivation that once propelled us forward, and instead begin looking for ways to cut our losses and retrieve the comforting feelings of security and certainty. This is the "failure zone," the place where our sense of purpose and dreams are most at risk.

We have two choices when we're in the failure zone: give up or persist. This chapter is all about how to do the latter, which brings us to its core concept: *One of the biggest barriers to our breakthrough success is ourselves.* Numerous external challenges will inevitably arise and surprise—the product, the service, the business model, customers, partners, distribution channels, the competition, or whatever else—but how we deal with our own responses to uncertainty, ambiguity, and fear can make the difference between long-term success and giving up prematurely. When we're passing through the failure zone, the goal is to take the surprise out of failure.

External Criticism Is Rooted in Old Assumptions

If you're reading this book on an Amazon Kindle, you probably already know that you're holding a breakthrough. From the start, many people believed the Kindle would transform the definition of a "book," not to mention stir up the publishing industry as a whole. But there were also naysayers who didn't think an online retailer had any business getting directly into consumer electronics. Jeff Bezos, Amazon.com's CEO, once described how criticism always arises around business breakthroughs: "Any time you do something big, that's disruptive, there will be critics." He went on to say, "There will be well-meaning critics who genuinely misunderstand what you are doing or genuinely have a different opinion. And there will be the self-interested critics that have a vested interest in not liking what you are doing and they will have reason to misunderstand." Bezos succinctly described Amazon's strategy for dealing with such criticism: "We are willing to be misunderstood for long periods of time."[48]

In 2003, *Time* magazine ranked iTunes as the "Coolest Invention" of the year. But in an article published shortly after that by *Fast Company*,[49] the magazine panned Apple for its lack of creativity. Here's a brief excerpt: "But even in that banner year, Apple's creative energy hasn't amounted to very much in financial terms. The father of the PC—and, remember, the industry's number-one vendor in 1980—has since sunk to a lowly ninth. . . . Sadly, Apple is also behind such no-namers as Acer (seventh) and Legend (eighth). So much for innovation and creativity." Even after Apple had reestablished itself with its iPod and sold more than 20 million songs through iTunes, *Fast Company* critiqued Apple on the basis of being a traditional *computer* company, not the broader company that it was rapidly evolving into (the one that has since introduced the iPhone and iPad and whose iTunes has now sold more than *10 billion* songs).

I don't know about you, but for most people getting publicly flogged by a prominent magazine like *Fast Company* might cause some serious doubts, or even a crisis of confidence. But like Bezos, Apple's founder, Steve Jobs, knew that this kind of pushback is only natural during the process of creating business breakthroughs that threaten the status quo. In a commencement speech he gave at Stanford University two years after the *Fast Company* article, Jobs gave that year's graduates a gift when he recommended they adopt one of the secrets to his success: "Don't let the noise of others' opinions drown out your own inner voice."[50]

The other day I spoke with Ellen Marram, someone who has a history of listening to her own voice. Ellen currently sits on the boards of Ford Motor Company, The New York Times, and Eli Lilly. But it wasn't her current work I was interested in. In an earlier career, Ellen did something that no one else had ever achieved on such a massive scale, and something that even people inside her organization said was impossible. She made a healthier cookie.

Whereas most of the initial criticism of the Kindle and the iPhone came from outside sources like analysts and the press, Ellen initially had to deal with naysayers inside her own organization, Nabisco, Inc. Ellen had just become President and CEO of Nabisco Biscuit Company, the largest unit of the corporation and the one known for its cookies like Oreos and Chips Ahoy. She came to that position after running another Nabisco business, one focused on healthy food alternatives. In the early 1990s, healthy eating was still pretty much on the fringe. So when Ellen announced that she wanted to launch a line of fat-free cookies, everyone thought she was crazy. At the source of all the resistance was the fact that people saw healthy cookies as the edible equivalent of cardboard, which was a pretty accurate description of the mealy cookies with carob chips found in the small health-food stores that existed at the time. Plus, they said, putting the words *healthy* and *cookie* together made an oxymoron that consumers simply wouldn't accept.

"Coming in from the outside, it was so obvious it was a huge opportunity, but no one else could see it," Ellen told me. A few people even hoped the market research would come back saying consumers hated the idea. Ellen pushed on, though, and managed to convince her bosses to give the idea a chance. She recalled Nabisco's CEO saying, "I thought Ellen was crazy but I had never seen her so absolutely convinced she was right." And right she was. Consumers loved SnackWells, the brand that established the "healthier snacking" trend of the 1990s and created an entirely new category of cookie.

In reflecting on her experience, Ellen remarked, "All organizations end up smoking their own exhaust. The real trap is when you start seeing the world from the inside out, rather than the outside in. You start believing the myths of the organization—of what it can do and should do." The skepticism and criticism that Ellen experienced weren't a personal attack on her. Everyone around her was simply blind to the opportunity because of their entrenched mindsets.

Steve Jobs said to stay focused on our inner voice. Jeff Bezos says we need to be willing to be misunderstood for long periods of time. Ellen Marram embraced both strategies. A balancing act is often required to know when to listen to others, and when to stop listening to the outside and tune in to the inside. Achieving business breakthroughs takes time, which often means we must put up with skepticism and criticism and push forward in the face of them. It becomes easier to forge on when we remember that critiques often come from old mindsets that haven't yet caught up with our new mental models. And it's also important to recognize that when others feel that their existing way of doing things is threatened, they will grasp at whatever they can to maintain their own sense of certainty and control—which often means tearing down our breakthroughs.

Questions to Consider

⊃ What do you typically do when you're feeling misunderstood by others?

⊃ How do you respond to skepticism and criticism?

➲ When have you been able to listen to yourself, even in the midst of being bombarded with criticism from others? How were you able to successfully keep out the noise, stay focused on your own inner voice, and keep going?

Failure Results from Fear, Not Failure Itself

To suggest that failure results from being fearful might sound either naive or crazy. So, bear with me for a moment. When we step back from it all, it becomes possible to view just about any failure as no more than a "setback" if taken in a broader context. Of course, some failures can be much more painful than others, and we can feel like they've just signaled the end of our world as we know it. And in some cases they do indeed represent the end of a project, a product, or even a company. But, by taking a longer-term view, we can start to view discrete failures as stepping-stones to something greater than what we just lost—whether it's on an individual level or from the perspective of a team or organization.

Real failure results only when we do one thing: give up. But there's a big problem we all share. When we're doing something extraordinarily difficult, we're *preconditioned* to give up. Yes, that's right. Our gut instinct is to submit to the urge to fail. It might sound extreme, but there's research that makes this very case, and it highlights why we need to do everything we can to push through the single most destructive emotion that most everyone shares: *fear*.

Jennifer Lerner is in touch with emotions. Lerner heads the Laboratory for Decision Science at Harvard University and is probably the world's leading expert on how emotions influence judgment and decisions. What's interesting about Lerner's work is that she's zeroed in on various feelings—anger, fear, pride, happiness—and discovered how each of these specifically affects our assessments of situations and our related decisions.

In one study,[51] Lerner and her colleagues examined people's inherent levels of fear. Their subjects indicated whether or not they were afraid of various situations or objects, such as being stuck in enclosed places or coming face to face with snakes. They also shared the extent to which they experienced a variety of day-to-day feelings, from being nervous to feeling like they were failures in life. What these researchers did next might sound a little morbid, but it makes a great point about the influence of fear. Lerner provided these same individuals with a list of twelve events that are known to cause fatalities each year in the United States, such as strokes, cancer, and floods. To give a reference point, Lerner told her subjects that 50,000 people die each year due to car accidents. She then asked her subjects to give estimates of the total number of annual fatalities for each of the twelve events. In this study and in others like it, Lerner and her colleagues found the same thing time and again: People who are most fearful in life provide consistently higher estimates of the number of fatalities than people who carry around other emotions.

Over the years, Lerner has reached a number of conclusions from this study and her broader research about fear and its connection to risk taking and decision making. The first is that most people's fear stems from two interrelated causes: uncertainty about the future and a sense of not being fully in control or able to influence how a given situation will unfold (or, said another way, the fear that they may be surprised).

Maybe all of this is pretty self-evident so far, but here's where it starts to get interesting. When people are fearful, they become more pessimistic in how they see the future—like when they give higher estimates of the number of fatalities. And here's the kicker. Lerner says that when it comes to decision making, this pessimism leads people to choose risk-averse options in order to create as much certainty as possible given their situations. That's exactly why during a falling stock market people dump their investments just as the market is hitting rock bottom in order to "get out." For many people, getting out of the market and losing their shirts provides a level of comfort that is still much better than living with the pain of uncertainty. Whether it's financial investing or creating a business breakthrough, our fears create pessimism about the future that in turn make us scramble to find certainty, which leads us to sacrifice the long-term view by replacing it with the quickest way out. And the way out often involves quitting.

The process of creating breakthroughs is chock-full of ambiguity and uncertainty. And the fear of failure is a natural reaction to these conditions. Eliminating that fear isn't as important as simply being aware of it and of how it can stifle us. Many of us conjure up scenarios about things that might happen or become fearful that we'll be surprised by something we can't anticipate. At a deeper level, it's all about control. If we believe we control something, we usually don't experience fear, since that thing is predictable and its future outcome is clear. When we feel out of control, even just a little bit, that's when the fear of failure is infused into our mindsets and decisions.

When we're holding onto the fear of failure—whether we're conscious of it or not—the energy we put into specifically avoiding failure limits our personal potential and the potential of our employees, teams, and organizations. Some people are quite attuned to their fear and know it when they see it. For others, it may show up in the form of physical stress or emotional edginess. Regardless, experiencing fear of failure can actually be worse than the potential failure itself, since it can prematurely stop us dead in our tracks. This is the biggest danger—giving in to our fear and allowing it to keep us from moving forward. Sure, we might avoid a crushing setback by doing so. But we'll also miss out on the chance to learn from that failure and use it as springboard to something greater.

Questions to Consider

- ➲ Think about a time when you felt great uncertainty. How did it feel? How was this uncertainty tied to a feeling of lack of control?

- ➲ When have you experienced fear of failure? What were the circumstances that led to that fear?

- ➲ When have you seen others fearful of failure, and how did their fear influence their behavior?

Reframing Failures as Stepping-Stones Keeps Us Going

At a recent Amazon shareholders' meeting, Jeff Bezos said that he expects his company to fail. These were his words: "I can guarantee you that everything we do will not work. And, I am never concerned about that. . . . A big piece of the story we tell ourselves about who we are, is that we are willing to invent. We are willing to think long-term."[52] One of the reasons Bezos is willing to fail is precisely because he's adopted a broad mindset. He has the view that everything that happens in the short term, whether a success or failure, is part of his longer-term journey. Sure, it may sound reasonable for the CEO of a market-leading, multi-billion-dollar company like Amazon to take this approach. But if you live in the corporate world, you know that this mindset is actually pretty rare. The importance of taking a broader view applies across the board, even to the smallest of organizations.

Allyson Phillips was one of the first recipients of Kimberly-Clark's Huggies MomInspired Grant Program that I discussed earlier. Allyson is the epitome of a "mompreneur." From the moment her first child was born, her entrepreneurial wheels began spinning. At the time of her daughter's birth, front-facing baby carriers were all the rage—the "reverse backpacks" that allow your baby to see the world while propped up tightly against your chest. Allyson saw a big unmet need for both parent and baby alike: a soft blanket-like cover for those carriers to protect children from the sun in the summer and keep them warm in the winter. Her mommy friends loved it, and so she was off to the races with what she felt was her million-dollar idea. To keep things in the family, she named her company Kiley Madison Inc., after her daughter.

After months of learning the ropes of textile manufacturing and immersing herself in the highly competitive $8-billion baby products market, something devastating happened. BabyBjörn, the company that makes the actual baby carriers Allyson was hoping to modify, started manufacturing and promoting their own version of her product. In a single instant, all of Allyson's dreams flew out the window. There was no way she could compete with such an established company. And, because Kiley Madison's primary product was the baby carrier blanket, Allyson was left with nothing to sell. Not surprisingly, she wondered whether she'd ever find another big idea and whether the business itself was even viable.

About the same time that Allyson was winding down her blanket business, she took her daughter to her playgroup. A toddler across the room was drinking from a sippy cup. The little girl had to throw her head back at a ninety-degree angle, mouth sucking to the sky, in order to finish her beverage. The motion threw the girl off balance and she toppled onto her backside and started to cry.

Allyson went home that night and slid a piece of cardboard into one of her daughter's sippy cups so that it formed an inverted slide inside the body of the cup. She filled the altered cup with Cheerios and discovered with delight that all of the cereal slid down easily and efficiently, without the need for the cup to go fully vertical. With that, the "Tilty Cup" was born.

Fast-forward to today. To sum it up, Allyson reinvented the "sippy cup." Her fast-selling product line is available in major national outlets like Babies"R"Us, One Step Ahead, and Amazon.com and has been featured in a variety of media, including *Parenting* magazine, *Contemporary Pediatrics* magazine, and even a "Got Milk?" advertisement. A little sippy cup might not sound like such a major contribution to the world, but it's amazing what a big difference something so small can make. What happened? Allyson didn't give up, that's what. She pushed through her numerous failures and used them as stepping-stones instead of experiencing them as brick walls.

"It's such a simple concept. One little addition took a regular sippy cup and made it worlds better," Allyson told me. And better it is. With traditional sippy cups, kids are trained to crane their heads back in a vertical position to drink, definitely not a normal position unless, of course, you're chugging a beer. The smallest kids lose their balance and fall over. And, more often than not, kids give a cup back saying it's empty when it's not because they simply can't get to the last drop. The Tilty Cup solves these issues and more.

"It's like training wheels for drinking," Allyson shared. "It actually helps with the transition to a regular cup. My son was able to drink from a regular cup sooner and without spilling because he learned the right way to drink from the start." Parents and pediatricians from all over the country are giving accolades to Tilty Cup for accelerating kids' development—and of course for saving them and their children from crying over spilt milk.

As is often the case, coming up with the initial idea for Tilty Cup was the easy part. But to hear Allyson tell the story of Tilty Cup, it's easy to see why her photo should be found in the dictionary under "roller coaster ride." "You start off and everyone tells you what a great idea you have," she said. "You think you're going to be a millionaire in a couple of days, but as you grow, you just have to keep putting more and more of yourself into it to make it work. There were definitely times when I wondered if it was all worth it."

First, Allyson paid $10,000 for a grand total of four plastic prototypes. These first cups worked wonderfully, but Allyson's husband, who picked them up from the manufacturer, forgot to pass on a key detail about their construction: They were not built to withstand warm liquids. The day before their first major trade show, Allyson went to the sink to wash them out and was horrified to feel them melting in her hands. Ten grand was quite literally washing away down the drain! "That was definitely a crying moment," she recalled. Fortunately not all of the prototypes were totally ruined and the show went on.

At the trade show, Allyson noticed several people circling the aisles and eyeing her booth. After she gave them a friendly smile and an invitation to come closer, she quickly understood why they'd kept their distance. They were from the baby products company Gerber, the competition. With apprehensive looks on their faces, they commented to Allyson, "We can't believe no one's thought of this before." With that indirect pat on the back, they went on their way. Given Allyson's former experience with BabyBjörn, she immediately feared another major company would beat her to the market. But she also knew that, based on the reaction she just saw, she was on to something big.

Soon after, a forty-foot-long truck packed with Tilty Cups arrived at the curb in front of Allyson's house in San Diego. The family unloaded the boxes by hand, placing them inside a curbside storage unit they had rented. This storage solution worked fine until the unthinkable happened: It rained in San Diego. The roof of the storage unit leaked, ru-ining thousands of dollars worth of inventory. Allyson and her husband slogged through the storm all night long transferring soggy boxes into their living room. "I remember looking at all of our neighbors' houses. They were dark and quiet. They were asleep and here we are in the rain with floodlights out and heaters on. It was horrendous."

Despite these tribulations, the elegantly simple solution of the Tilty Cup caught on. Allyson and her husband went from being ec-static with shipping a few units at a time to a whole new dilemma: too much success too fast. You'd think that with all their sales, Allyson would be in hog heaven. But managing large inventories requires significant upfront investment, the scope of which they hadn't fully anticipated. They actually ran out of their inventory at one point, a mistake that almost killed the company. "It was devastating to have to tell the buyer at Amazon we couldn't send them a new batch of prod-ucts for four months," she told me. "I was really afraid they'd just can-cel their order altogether." Just at the time Allyson was struggling with financing their next large container of products—and in the midst of a potential revolt from her distributors—she received a call letting her know she had just been awarded the $15,000 mompreneur grant from Kimberly-Clark. Talk about a pleasant surprise.

Allyson's story highlights how reframing failure can give us the juice to keep going. When we look at a particular failure as a stepping-stone to something even greater out there, we're able to push through our knee-jerk instincts to give up. Think about all of the opportunities Allyson had to call it quits. She could have thrown in the towel after wrapping up her blanket business. She could have bailed out of the trade show after losing her prototypes. She could have given up the moment those Gerber representatives noticed her product, fearing that her fledgling idea would be knocked off by the behemoth corporation. Then, after all that, she easily could have lost faith when she ran out of inventory and a new shipment was nowhere in sight. But she didn't. She looked at these various surprises and failures as stepping-stones. Even though sometimes these stones hurt her feet, she kept stepping on them anyway, knowing they were part of the larger path to success.

Questions to Consider

- ➲ Think about a time when you "failed." What happened, and why did you consider it "failure"? What did you learn? How did you move on?

- ➲ Think about a time when you took a step back and put your day-to-day challenges into a larger context. What did that do for you?

- ➲ When have you been able to view a failure as a setback rather than the end of the world? How did doing this help you, your team, or your organization?

- ➲ As you look back on whatever failures you've experienced, how can you reinterpret them to uncover the stepping-stones that led to something bigger later down the line?

Optimism Fuels Action

There are big benefits to modifying our mindsets to view things in a larger context, as opposed to looking at a single activity, a painful setback, or the prospect of a failure as the end of the line. Some of this has to do with staying optimistic, since, as we've seen from the research, when we're in the failure zone it's easy to lose hope. Once we start to believe that the future holds more peril than promise, it becomes that much more challenging to push through to the other side. Understanding the dynamics of optimism is a good starting point, but an additional ingredient is essential: action. Talking the talk of optimism is all well and good, but we have to walk the walk as well.

Suzanne Segerstrom is a researcher at the University of Kentucky and one of the foremost authorities on optimism. In fact, she wrote an entire book on how optimistic people get what they want out of their lives.[53] To Segerstrom, the essence of optimism is believing that the future will more likely be good rather than bad. As a result, she says that "optimists believe their goals are achievable," and because of this, "they don't give up easily." Her conclusions are backed up by research.[54] In one study, people were tested and classified as either optimists or pessimists. They were then given a set of anagrams and told to unscramble them (for example, the letters "potrumec" had to be unscrambled to spell "computer"). What no one knew was that one of the anagrams was impossible; the scrambled letters couldn't be reorganized into a meaningful word. While optimists spent more than 20 percent longer than pessimists trying to solve the anagrams overall, they spent twice as much time working to solve the impossible anagram than did the pessimists. Basically, optimists showed a greater propensity for persistence—they didn't give up as quickly as the pessimists.

Segerstrom summarizes her years of research by saying, "The longer I have studied optimism, the more I have come to believe that the benefits of optimism are only partially from *being* optimistic. That is, having optimistic beliefs gets you only so far. You have to get the rest of the way through *doing*." In an interview with *Psychology Today*,[55] Segerstrom elaborated on this by saying that "optimism's benefits have less to do with mood and much more to do with persistence."

The persistence that Segerstrom describes is what others have called "grounded optimism" (as opposed to "blind optimism," which involves naively convincing oneself that only good things can ever happen). For example, Jonathan Haidt, a psychologist at the University of Virginia, says that grounded optimists "alternate between active coping and reappraisal. If active coping fails to fix the problem, they reappraise the situation, looking for hidden benefits, and, invested with flexibility, write a new chapter."[56] Said another way, grounded optimists deal with the setbacks and surprises that are thrown at them by looking for hidden meanings so they can assess trade-offs to quickly get clear on their next step.

When I was doing the research for this book, I almost dismissed the literature on optimism, since I had assumed that optimism was simply a personality trait. What I eventually found surprised me. Just like we're preconditioned to give up when the going really gets tough, we're also wired to overcome this preconditioning, provided we do the right things.

Conrad Hilton, founder of Hilton Hotels, once remarked that "successful people keep moving. They make mistakes, but they don't quit." Through "keeping moving," our actions themselves create a self-reinforcing feedback loop, something I call "the persistence cycle." When we take action, we see results, learn from them, and modify our assumptions and behaviors based on these results—similar to what we discussed in the preceding chapter. As a result, we can identify progress even when something we've done doesn't work out as planned. Good results can be celebrated, while bad results can be seen as learning opportunities. This mental framework further feeds our optimism and inspires us to take additional action, which begins the persistence cycle again.

Pushing through the failure zone requires starting and accelerating a persistence cycle. For many people and teams, getting over the hump to take a first step once the feelings of uncertainty begin

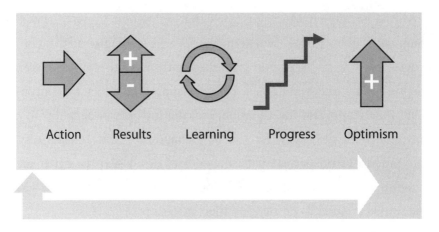

Persistence Cycle

is the difference between forging ahead and spiraling down. When we're paralyzed, even a small step can feel like we're climbing Mt. Everest. But the good news is that there's a secret to how anyone can jump-start the persistence cycle.

Have you ever heard the saying "Fake it until you make it"? Usually it's used in jest to convey the idea that forcing ourselves to act confidently even when we're not feeling that way gets us moving and eventually leads to success. There's actually something to this idea, and recent research confirms it.

In one study jointly conducted by researchers from Columbia and Harvard Universities,[57] people were placed into two groups. No one was told what the experiment was about, but everyone had electrocardiogram (ECG) electrodes placed on their chests to fake them into thinking that the experiment was related to physiology. One group was told to position their bodies in two different "high-power poses" (like kicking back in a chair with feet perched on a desk) for one minute each, while the other was asked to assume two submissive "low-power poses." After doing this, all participants were given

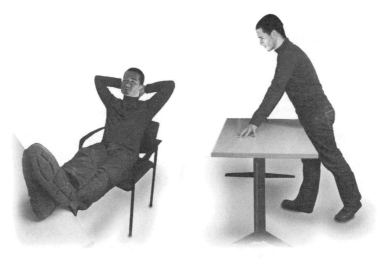

High-Power Poses

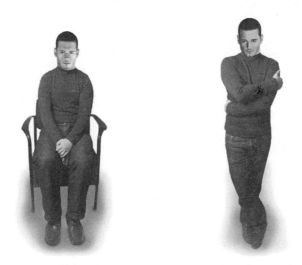

Low-Power Poses

Reprinted by Permission of SAGE Publications[58]

$2 each and told they could either keep it or risk it all by rolling dice in order to double their money (the odds of winning were 50/50). They were also given a survey to measure how "powerful" and "in charge" they felt after the experiment.

The researchers found that significantly more of the "high-power posers" gambled their money and reported feelings of being powerful and in charge. The "low-power posers" took less risk and didn't feel as powerful. And here's something even more interesting: The researchers collected saliva samples from all participants immediately before and after the experiment in order to measure their "neuroendrocrine" levels of testosterone (a hormone linked to feelings of power and dominance) and cortisol (a hormone tied to stress, hypertension, and decreased immune functioning). After comparing hormone levels before and after the experiment, the researchers found that the two groups differed substantially. The high-power posers showed a significant increase in testosterone with a decrease in cortisol, whereas the low-power posers had *decreases* in testosterone and *increases* in cortisol. Neuroendrocrine levels don't lie. Simply acting powerful leads to real physical changes and a feeling of *being* powerful. Feeling powerful increases the likelihood of acting that way—like challenging the status quo by taking risks.

In another study led by William Fleeson at Wake Forest University,[59] researchers brought a bunch of college students into a lab and asked them to participate in two ten-minute group discussions. In one discussion they were told to act extroverted (assertive, bold, and energetic), and in the other they were instructed to act introverted (reserved and passive). Just about everyone said they had more fun and were happier when they acted extroverted. The researchers asked another group of students to track and report back their behavior and feelings each week for ten weeks. The results were similar to those of the earlier study. Extroverted behaviors, such as "singing out loud to a song on the radio, walking over to an attractive person and talking to them, asking a question in class or voicing an opinion," all positively influenced the subjects' moods. In fact, across the board, 100 percent of participants were statistically happier when acting extroverted than introverted. And this wasn't simply a function of people acting out their natural tendencies. Importantly, Fleeson noted that "even introverts can act extroverted and become happier by changing their behavior."

These studies shed light on the mechanics behind the persistence cycle. The implication for what we can do to start pushing through our times of doubt is simple—figure out another small step and just take it. It really doesn't even matter what it is as long as it feels assertive and generally in the right direction. Then, do it again.

Questions to Consider

- ➲ How have you seen your own optimism or pessimism influence your ability to move forward to address a challenge or pursue an opportunity?

- ➲ Have you ever "faked it until you made it?" What happened?

- ➲ When have you learned something new that energized you in a way that kept you moving forward?

Making It Real

We talked about how failure is inevitable when we create business breakthroughs. We explored research that outlines how fear makes us more risk averse and likely to give up on our pursuits. We looked at the benefits of reframing failure as stepping-stones in a longer journey. And we learned about the different ways that we can push back on old mindsets, including the willingness to be misunderstood for long periods of time and the need to keep ourselves grounded in our own voice rather than reacting to outside critiques. And, finally, we reviewed the importance of action in fueling optimism and creating the persistence required for pushing through the failure zone.

The goal of the fourth step of the leapfrogging life cycle is to take the surprise out of failure. Said another way, the goal is to push the whole idea of failure itself into the background. When we make failure a relative and natural experience, any "negative surprises" we encounter become the foundational stepping-stones that guide us forward. With this mindset, we're armed to push through the failure zone.

 ## Leapfrogging Tools

1. Find Your Future Failure

As we discussed, fear of failure can really get in the way of breakthroughs. One way to combat our fears is to hit them head-on. Based on your aspirations and goals, consider what you think would be the biggest possible failure you could experience. Explore the scenario by playing out the event, the impact it would have, the implications for your organization, and how you—individually, as a team, or as an organization—would respond in both the short and long terms. Consider the following questions:

- What does your most disastrous scenario look like?
- What impact would this worst-case scenario have on individuals, teams, the organization, customers, partners, and other stakeholders?

- What would be the short-term impact on you personally? What would be the long-term impact?

- If this scenario became a reality, what would you personally feel or experience?

- How could you rebound from this failure? What would you do next?

- In what ways could the failure be used as a stepping-stone to something else?

Now that you have explored your biggest future failure, step back and consider what insights you gained from this activity. What new alternatives or options opened up? Did any of your assumptions or feelings about failure change?

2. Get Controlling

The source of most fear is a feeling of lack of control. More often than not, we're unaware of this deeper source of our fears. By making a list of things we control versus those we don't control, we can uncover the very things that can lead us to experience stress, anxiety, and fear. Create a bullet point list of the things you control and those you don't control related to your breakthrough.

Things We Can Control	Things We Cannot Control

Once you have your list, explore the following questions:

- For the things that you **don't** control:
  - ❑ What are the common characteristics, patterns, or dynamics of the things that you don't control?
  - ❑ Which could have the most positive or negative impact on your breakthrough?
  - ❑ What is the underlying uncertainty in relation to these things? How does this uncertainty affect you?
  - ❑ How can you best "stay close" to these things so you can track how they are unfolding over time?
  - ❑ Which things cause the greatest fear? Why?
  - ❑ Which things are less of a concern? Why?
- For the things that you **do** control:
  - ❑ What are the common characteristics, patterns, or dynamics of the things that you do control?
  - ❑ Which of these things provide you with the greatest feeling of direction and confidence? Why?
  - ❑ In what ways can you apply the characteristics of these things to create greater certainty in the things that you don't control?

3. Jump-Start the Persistence Cycle

Launching ourselves into the unknown can be intimidating, but that's exactly what's needed to jump-start the persistence cycle. Make a list of the biggest two or three unresolved questions related to your breakthrough. Determine the potential small steps

you could take to start addressing or resolving each one. Use the
following template:

Big Question #1	Actions to Address Big Question #1
Big Question #2	**Actions to Address Big Question #2**
Big Question #3	**Actions to Address Big Question #3**

Once you have your list, prioritize the actions based on
which steps are easiest to take. Select the easiest one and do it.
Keep going down the list. Repeat this activity as needed.

8

Seize:
Make the Journey Part of the (Surprising) Destination

The key to realizing a dream is to focus not on success but on significance—and then even the small steps and little victories along your path will take on greater meaning.

—Oprah Winfrey

Chapter Eight Key Messages

1. Looking back, we see that every step was in the right direction.
2. Humility is the door to "predictable surprise."
3. Clarity of purpose is the ever-present guidepost.
4. "Telescoping" keeps us agile and adaptive.

It was never my intention to write a book about the "zen" of leap-frogging. But one thing continually struck me during my research for this book. Most of the people I spoke with saw their break-through success as resulting from literally everything that they had experienced—the intentional strategies and plans, the serendipitous surprises, the failures, and the wins along the way. Although some people told me that they might do things differently given the chance, most fully acknowledged that they couldn't have achieved what they did if they hadn't gone through the entire experience.

This brings us to the last phase of the leapfrogging life cycle. After pushing through the failure zone, we really start to see the fruits of our labor. The voices of the naysayers get softer. Outside recognition and support begin to flow. Little achievements snowball into bigger wins. Optimism grows. Now is the time to seize upon everything that's led us to where we are today.

The core message of this chapter is this: *When we experience our journey as part of our destination, we become agile and adaptive, able to respond to and deliver surprise as a natural part of who we are.* We can now seize upon our circumstances and take things to the next level. This chapter highlights the mindsets and behaviors that allow us to fully capitalize on our experiences and realize our business breakthroughs.

Surprise!—Looking Back, We See That Every Step Was in the Right Direction

Tena Clark founded and runs DMI Music in Los Angeles. Unlike most LA music producers, DMI's goal isn't to sell top-40 songs on iTunes. DMI is the world's leading "audio branding" and "music strategy" company, with clients that include Delta Air Lines, Cisco Systems, Build-A-Bear Workshop, and General Mills. DMI produces custom radio shows tailored for specific audiences and businesses, like General Mills's *Serving Up Soul* syndicated radio program that's played in fifty markets around the United States as a way for the company to connect to the thirty-five- to fifty-year-old African American female market. And, if you've ever flown on an airline and listened to the in-flight music on your headphones, you've probably

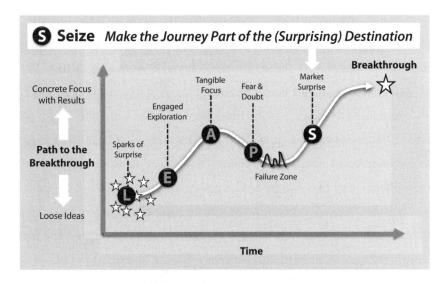

Seize Phase of the Leapfrogging Life Cycle

heard one of DMI's customized programs. But perhaps Tena Clark's favorite work involves creating "audio logos," like the one she crafted for United Airlines, which has made the first few notes of Gershwin's *Rhapsody in Blue* synonymous with the airline. That little riff is such an integral part of United's identity that it's impossible to hear those notes without thinking of the airline.

Tena's story embodies the "journey is the destination" experience. Tena didn't just dream up her business breakthrough out of the clear blue sky. It was forged over years, through a whole series of different jobs, ideas, trials, and errors. When she told me about her path to success, I could just see the puzzle pieces falling into place. But even Tena admits that she didn't know what the big picture would look like until all those pieces came together. "The only thing I knew starting out was that I wanted to create music and use music to connect people together," she told me in her folksy Mississippi drawl. "But I never knew I would find so many ways to do it."

Beginning at age five, Tena would visit New Orleans to listen to music with her mother, a big-band songwriter. Ten years after her first visit, Tena played drums in her first professional gig, which led to tours with bands all over the Southeast as a drummer. Her travels eventually took her out west to Los Angeles, where she began to write theme songs and music for movies and television shows. To make ends meet, she also penned a few advertising jingles on the side. When the Leo Burnett ad agency approached Tena to work on their McDonald's account, she gladly took the job. This little gig turned into a big break in more ways than one: Tena created the instantly recognizable national campaign theme "Have You Had Your Break Today," propelling her songwriting into the mainstream in a way she could never have imagined.

A by-product of writing jingles in an ad agency was that she received a default crash course in marketing and branding. So, in the late 1990s Tena realized that the music industry faced tumultuous change. Tena knew she could either remain a successful songwriter within the establishment or forge a new path using the cracks created by the Internet as windows of opportunity. She decided to combine her love of music with her newfound business acumen, and so she founded DMI.

Tena says her present-day success is the combined result of all of her stops along the way that, together, gave her the right mixture of ideas and experiences to achieve her breakthrough. "It's amazing, you do this thing, you meet this person and you don't think much about it but then two years down the line, five years down the line, they become an integral part of your life or something you're creating. It seems crazy but it happens all the time," she told me. Today DMI has nearly 100 employees and works with some of the biggest names in the corporate world. It still programs in-flight radio for United Airlines and other carriers—including Air Force One. Not bad for a drummer from a small town in Mississippi.

Just like Tena's story, many of the other examples I've shared show how our aggregate experiences add up to where we are, here and now. Whether we've experienced successes, failures, or positive or negative surprises, we're all a product of our own history, while at the same time we contain the seeds to transform it. In a sense, the goal is to merge the "past and present" with the "present and future"—to understand that everything we do builds upon the past but that nothing is constrained by the past.

Past experiences taken by themselves may not seem extraordinarily significant. But when we look at the collection of our experiences together, the synergies between seemingly disparate events can be quite surprising. Steve Jobs captured the essence of this idea when he said "You can't connect the dots looking forward; you can only connect them looking backwards. So you have to trust that the dots will somehow connect in your future."[60] Here's another brief example to further illustrate this point. This story is about vegetables.

By now, most people know about celebrity chefs like Rachael Ray, Alain Ducasse, and Nora Pouillon. But what if I told you there was such a thing as a "celebrity gardener"? (And no, I don't mean the guy who trims Tom Cruise's hedges.) Asafumi Yamashita has definitely earned the title.

In the backyard of his home outside of Paris, Yamashita grows exquisite Japanese vegetables like *hinona* and *kabu* for some of the best restaurants in the world. In fact, he keeps a waiting list of chefs dying to cook with his prized ingredients. But he sells only to the ones he believes will do justice to the food. That's right:

Yamashita forces people to prove themselves worthy before they can buy his veggies.

"I have no interest in selling my turnips to a cook who will make duck with turnips—it's too banal," Yamashita once told *W* magazine. "I prefer to sell them to geniuses like Pierre Gagnaire or Eric Briffard who are much more creative."[61]

You might think someone as gifted at—and deadly serious about—growing food would have been tending the soil since childhood. But you'd be wrong. Pardon the pun, but Yamashita is the ultimate late bloomer. When he first came to Paris from Tokyo at the age of twenty-two, Yamashita wanted to become an artist or perhaps a musician. He studied art and played the drums around the city for a few years, then went back to Tokyo and tried his hand at the import-export business. He didn't come back to France for more than a decade. It was the late 1980s. Sushi and other Japanese food were becoming popular—as was another export from Yamashita's native country, bonsai trees. As a child, Yamashita had learned from his father how to tend the miniature conifers. So, to make a living, he started raising them at his house and leasing them to Japanese restaurants around Paris. Then one day a chef at one of the restaurants suggested he should grow some Japanese produce as well. Yamashita decided to give it a try. He flew back to Japan and bought his first batch of seeds.

Yamashita soon realized he was onto something—and not just because restaurants started fighting over the rights to his harvests. All of the interests and skills he had accumulated throughout his life combined to make him an extraordinary gardener. His experience in the import-export business helped him to bring the best seeds over from Japan. His love of art gave him an appreciation for the growing process and the beauty of his creations. And his work with bonsai taught him the meticulousness and patience he needed to cultivate the kind of produce that would make even the world greatest chefs' mouths water. All of these seemingly independent happenings came together at an unexpected intersection that Yamashita knew he must pursue. With such a pedigree and blend of skills, it's no wonder that he can charge a premium for his fare. Yamashita's micro-tomatoes sell for $40 a pound!

Tena's and Yamashita's stories about music and vegetables couldn't be more different. But they both highlight the blindingly obvious 20-20 hindsight that we have when we look backward from breakthrough success. As many of the other examples I've shared demonstrate, everything that we experience makes important contributions to our breakthroughs, even the bumps in the road. The challenge is to internalize this mindset and then to embrace the highs and the lows as equally essential elements of our journeys while we're experiencing them. When we can do this, we open ourselves up to surprising new possibilities.

Questions to Consider

- ➲ Look back and consider various events that may have seemed unrelated at the time but have actually come together to bring you to where you are today. What connections do you see?

- ➲ What is surprising about how things have come together from the past to shape your current journey? What does this tell you?

Humility Opens Us Up to Seeing Surprise

Jin Kwon, the South Korean martial arts master, once said: "In the process of trial and error, our failed attempts are meant to destroy arrogance and provoke humility." The feelings of uncertainty and doubt that are inherent in the failure zone are the very things that help us achieve a new perspective. When we push through to the other side, we're able to look back and see that we didn't know what we didn't know—but that we're now smarter than ever. We're humbled because we acknowledge that we didn't have all the answers, or even the right questions. This realization is especially powerful when it goes along with the recognition that we once thought we knew it all. The experience of humility creates an enhanced receptivity to seeing surprises and seizing upon them to move forward.

When I asked Chuck Templeton, founder of OpenTable, what enabled him to overcome the early challenges of his start-up, he said with a smirk, "Ignorance was bliss." Allyson Phillips from Tilty Cup readily admitted that she didn't know how hard it would be to launch her line of baby products. Gloria Montenegro de Chirouze told me she expected her Parisian café, Caféotheque, to take off within two years—but it took five. And Mike Feinberg, founder of KIPP Academies, was once quoted as saying, "We didn't know what we didn't know. . . . No one said how impossible this was going to be."

The lesson I've taken from these candid quotes is this: Big things often have humble roots, and I don't just mean that they start small. One of the most important things that can open doors to the power of surprise is humility. Perhaps the best starting point for understanding how valuable humility can be is to look at its opposite—narcissism.

In a research study conducted at the University of Amsterdam,[62] researchers looked at the impact of narcissism on team decision making and performance. Conventional wisdom suggests that traits like confidence, dominance, authority, and high self-esteem contribute to make great leaders. But the researchers found that this perception doesn't match reality—the narcissistic egos of people with these traits get in the way when it comes to listening to others and fostering the type of information exchange that leads to better ideas and decisions.

In the study, fifty groups of three people were each asked to select a fictitious job candidate. Forty-five pieces of information were provided to each group, with some information given to each person while other information was spread out across the triad and given to only a single person. One person in each triad was randomly assigned to be the group's leader. Everyone else was told that they could contribute information and advice but that the leader would be responsible for making the final decision.

The experiment was designed to ensure that the group could pick the best candidate only if all the information was shared, including those pieces of information that only one person possessed. If all the information didn't come out, the group would be led to select a less optimal job candidate. Following the activity, the participants completed surveys to measure their levels of narcissism and their perception of their leader's overall effectiveness in helping their group complete its task.

Across the board, the *most narcissistic* leaders were rated by their group members as the most *effective*—their dominant styles were seen as making them the best leaders. But there was a major disconnect between this perception and reality. The big egos of these top-ranked leaders didn't correlate with the best decisions. In fact, their teams consistently selected the *worst* job candidates. So what does this tell us?

Big egos stifle openness. When we're driven by our egos, our ability to remain open to outside inputs is severely limited. When we're overly concerned with being on center stage, maintaining control, or ensuring that our ideas are the only ones that get traction, we lose the opportunity to broaden our perspectives to see new possibilities.

The CEO of BzzAgent, Dave Balter, recently became a self-appointed ambassador for humility. His company started out like gangbusters, receiving millions of dollars in venture funding, and even graced the cover of *The New York Times Magazine*. But within a few short years, it hit hard times and had to cut 50 percent of its workforce. Balter freely admits that his big ego led to BzzAgent's downfall, and he credits a newfound humility for reviving the company. He even goes around speaking to other leaders about the downside of oversized egos. "Recognize [that] your place in the universe is no more important than anyone else's," Balter says to new CEOs. "Humility will prepare you for the endurance test to come."[63]

If we're interested in letting surprises walk into our organizations and our lives, we need to do things that leave the door wide open for them. There's not much formal research on the topic of humility out there, but here's the essence of what we need to do to embrace it:

- Be able to accurately assess our abilities and achievements.
- Acknowledge our imperfections, knowledge gaps, and limitations.
- Listen to new ideas, conflicting information, and advice from others.
- Keep our accomplishments in perspective.

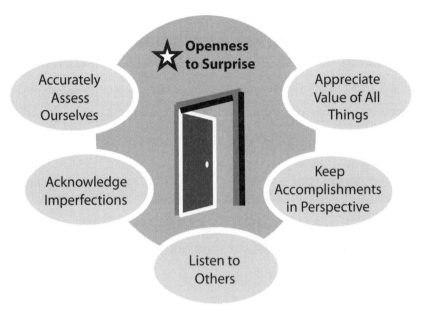

Humility and Openness to Surprise

- Appreciate the value of everything, including the various ways that people and things contribute to the world.[64]

When I spoke with Barbara Talbott, the former marketing executive of Four Seasons, she actually used the word *humility* to describe the secret to what kept her and her team going during the transformation of the hotel's brand. Because their egos weren't committed to a particular path, they were able to find surprises and then shift on a dime. They recognized that they didn't yet know "the answer" and that there probably wasn't a single one anyway. This allowed them to remain open to input and ideas from any and all sources and to let things unfold naturally as new information and knowledge surfaced, rather than fighting to push a preconceived agenda. Had they had such an agenda, their egos may have been tightly attached to it, which could have caused them to push back on their surprises rather than embrace them as they did. To be sure, humility isn't required for financial success. There are a lot of very successful people in the world who have huge egos. But if we want to tap into the power of surprise, humility opens the door while ego keeps it shut.

Questions to Consider

⮑ In what areas do you already have some degree of humility, and where do you still need to temper your ego?

⮑ In what ways do you think your ego closes the door on your ability to remain open to surprise?

Clarity of Purpose Is the Ever-Present Guidepost

I recently spoke with Massimo d'Amore, Mehmood Khan, and Sarah Robb O'Hagan, three major-league corporate executives who, together, are working to breathe life back into one of the biggest brands in the beverage world, Gatorade. A few years back, the orange staple of sidelines and locker rooms—owned by its parent company PepsiCo— started losing market share in a big way. Waves of consumers were bailing on traditional beverages and jumping on the iced tea, coffee, and Red Bull bandwagons.

The story begins with Massimo, President of PepsiCo's Global Bevereage Group and a consumer packaged goods veteran. Massimo recognized that whatever the solution to Gatorade's gargantuan challenge was, it couldn't be business as usual. So what did he do? He went out and hired Sarah, a sports marketing executive from Nike. Massimo initially received a lot of flak for this decision. "What was he doing hiring a shoe salesperson to run a billion-dollar beverage brand?" people questioned. But Massimo knew he needed to go outside in order to shake up the inside—and in this case, he was infusing a radically different perspective into the leadership mix.

Massimo, Mehmood, and Sarah approached the challenge from different angles, but all share the view that they're on a journey and that their success so far is fundamentally the result of a renewed clarity of purpose for the brand. The three recognized that the downturns in the economy were partly to blame for the drop in sales, but they also identified a larger, more important issue: At more than forty years old, Gatorade was starting to show its age.

Mehmood, PepsiCo's Chief Scientific Officer, is a medical doctor with extensive experience in clinical medicine and academic research. "I used to play a lot of squash and racquetball when I was a college student in the 1970s," Mehmood recalled. "My rackets back then were made of bamboo and sheep's gut. Nowadays, they are made of alloys, resins, and carbon fiber. And yet Gatorade looked the same, both inside and out."

Sarah, now Gatorade's President, knew the brand needed to evolve and pitched a radical first step—shortening Gatorade's iconic name to "G." To everyone's surprise, she also said that the company had to go "backward" first to find the best way forward. For years, PepsiCo had broadened Gatorade's appeal by selling it to a wider and wider market. But by trying to make it another drink option competing with the likes of Coke, fruit juice, and iced tea, the company had sacrificed the brand's identity as a scientifically proven sports nutrition product. Sarah wanted G to find itself again by refocusing on that original core group of consumers—athletes.

With Massimo's leadership, Sarah's business team and Mehmood's R&D group joined forces and cooked up a new recipe for the brand. Getting back in touch with Gatorade's roots meant tying the purpose of Gatorade to the purpose of athletes, which meant doing whatever it could to enhance overall performance. And to really understand what "performance" meant from the athletes' point of view, they went out and spoke to a number of their trusted advisors—from coaches, to trainers, to world-class athletes like Serena Williams, to everyday athletes in high schools. These discussions led them to see that their new emphasis on performance implied much more than treating Gatorade as a refreshing beverage to compensate for sweating during workouts. Homing in on the core purpose of Gatorade meant that they needed to look at exercise and sports performance in a whole new way—as a process rather than as an event.

The teams came up with a host of sports nutrition products to help athletes more effectively "prime" (get ready for) and "recover" from their sporting activities. "01 Prime" included a carbohydrate loaded pre-workout drink in a convenient pouch. "02 Perform" products included what we all know as traditional Gatorade. The post-workout "03 Recover" line included a protein recovery beverage designed to rebuild tired muscles. The line became known as the G Series. In addition, the teams created a small marketing group called "Mission Control," a dedicated team that uses Facebook, Twitter, and other social media to connect and communicate with athletes of all types on a daily basis to ensure that Gatorade maintains its laserlike focus. Indeed, identifying their core purpose—aiding athletes in as many ways as possible—unleashed an incredible amount of creative energy. Pretty soon they were dreaming up dozens of new products and strategies to support the holistic process of athletic performance.

Needless to say, many people in the company found this whole idea counterintuitive and controversial. If sales were dropping, they reasoned, shouldn't Gatorade be reaching out to a broader customer base instead of targeting such a seemingly small demographic? Wouldn't a retrenched focus on hard-core athletes alienate all the grocery stores, convenience stores, and other mass-market distributors of the product—not to mention all the moms who put Gatorade into their kids' lunches? Despite the internal skeptics, Massimo, Sarah, and Mehmood agreed that they had to go back to what they knew was the essence of the brand, and they firmly believed that performance was at the heart of Gatorade. But they also knew that they needed to back up their belief by getting their new products out the door and proving them in the market.

At the same time they were introducing the new Prime and Recover products, Sarah woke up to a brutal *Wall Street Journal* headline: *Pepsi Sweats Over Gatorade: CEO Nooyi Concedes Sports Drink's Glory Days Are Over; Redesign Backfires.* Most executives (hell, most human beings) would have wilted in the white-hot glare of that kind of media heat. "That was such a rocky year," Sarah recalled. "There was so much nervousness in the company and we had a lot of negative feedback from the media. But, at the same time, we were watching the good things that were starting to be said about our new products online with young athletes on Facebook and Twitter, and we could see that there was real energy building around our focus on performance." She also believed in the pipeline of things to come that she hoped would soon turn the critics into believers. To this day, Sarah keeps a copy of the *Wall Street Journal* article on her wall. It serves as a memento of sorts, a symbol of what she and everyone else involved in the project had to overcome as they searched their corporate souls for direction.

Today, the initial G Series line is further expanding with additions of products aimed at specific athletes, including fitness athletes and endurance athletes. The corporation continues to put its muscle behind Gatorade's marketing and product development, convinced now that "performance" is the ticket to success. In reflecting on Gatorade's journey, Massimo told me, "We were wandering in the forest and had lost the path. Our book is not finished yet, since we're still learning how to do this, but having rediscovered Gatorade's core purpose has helped all of our teams transition from operating as 'just another beverage' to becoming a real provider of overall sports nutrition, and this is our future."

Mehmood also reflected on their continuing journey and cited his experience as a doctor as a key factor in his ability to trust their joint instincts during the hard times. "The first time I put a cardiac pace wire in somebody's heart, I didn't tell them that it was my first time until after the operation. I tried to bring that same kind of confidence to this transformation. Sure you have doubts. But one thing I learned as a doctor, no matter how much doubt you have, when you take up that scalpel, you have to put those doubts aside and just trust in the purpose of why you're there."

When the skeptics are coming at us, it's very easy to lose our sense of purpose. As the great comedian Bill Cosby once said, "I don't know the key to success, but the key to failure is trying to please everybody." Massimo, Sarah, and Mehmood pushed aside the criticism by anchoring themselves and their teams in a strong sense of purpose. As they gained traction, their confidence grew and spread throughout the organization. Once they recognized that athletic performance was the key to reviving Gatorade, their decisions became easier and their creativity spiked. Their sense of purpose allowed them to filter out external noise while tuning in to their own internal guideposts. Here's another example of how clarity of purpose provides direction, but this time from a company much smaller than PepsiCo.

Rob Kalin doesn't necessarily seem like the kind of person who could fundamentally change the way people buy and sell things. He favors thrift-shop duds to three-piece suits. And, with his boyish face and strawberry blond hair, he looks a lot closer to eighteen than his real age of thirty. But don't let the slacker facade fool you. For the last six years, the founder of Etsy.com has been breaking all the rules for how business is conducted—and making an old-fashioned profit in the process.

In 2005, Kalin had an idea. He wanted to create a kind of on-line Bizarro World Walmart. Instead of hawking mass-produced goods at cut-rate prices, he set out to give people a space where they could save money on high-quality, one-of-a-kind products by buying directly from the artisans who had made them. Think of it as a crafts fair, only on a worldwide scale. But Kalin's goal wasn't just to let people score some cool handmade earrings or dresses. He was out to turn the whole concept of a globalized economy on its head by using its benefits—free trade and easy communication—to subvert what everyone assumed was its inevitable downsides. "Instead of having an economy dictate the behavior of communities," he told *The Wall Street Journal*, he wanted "to empower communities to dictate the behavior of economies."[65]

Today, some 400,000 jewelers, bookbinders, quilters, clothes makers, and other "hobbypreneurs" sell their creations on his website. Kalin says that $1,000 in goods is sold every second on Etsy.[66] Most items cost about twenty bucks, although some—like custom wedding gowns—are a lot more expensive. The only thing they all have in com-mon is that they're being sold by the folks who crafted them. There are no factories, no middlemen, no distribution networks; just the cus-tomer and the creator. All proceeds, minus Etsy's modest listing fee, go straight to the source. "We want to allow the makers of the world to claim authorship for what they're making," Kalin told *Inc.* magazine. "This is what Etsy stands for: the little guy being able to organize a better marketplace."[67]

Throughout this nonstop period of growth, including some major backing by venture capitalists, Kalin has faced a persistent paradox: how to keep an organization that has succeeded so fantastically by helping "the little guy" from losing its soul and becoming another faceless big company itself. He's dealt with this potential problem by actively anchoring Etsy in its core purpose, the thing that has made it so successful and one of a kind. He constantly reminds his staff that they are building something unique and special, too, just like the artisans who use their service. "Etsy itself is hundreds of thousands of very small businesses and I want to be able to keep that intimacy within our own company, even as we grow and the number of people we need to support grows," said Kalin. "It means always keeping a human face on what we're doing. I don't want to hide behind a corporate firewall and start speaking with some third-person voice. I want to always speak with a human voice."[68]

If you've ever been to the Etsy website, you know that Kalin's dedication to these values is unmistakable. The site profiles the artisans who are the core of what makes the Etsy economy go around. It highlights community events across the country. It helps people organize into "teams" so that they can meet, pool resources, and collaborate to make even better arts and crafts. The website exudes Kalin's purpose and is the front end of how Kalin runs the back end of his business—by keeping things human.

Many of the other examples I've shared demonstrate this same clarity of purpose. Barbara Talbott from Four Seasons led her company onto the web by ensuring that her new website extends to its guests all of the attributes of the "Four Seasons experience." With this clear goal firmly established, it became easier for her and her team to filter in and filter out an overwhelming number of ideas and design options for the site. Similarly, Yamashita's sense of purpose keeps him focused on the impeccable quality and craftsmanship of his vegetables. Given his success and the overwhelming demand for his products, most people would be tempted to expand. But Yamashita keeps his operation intentionally backyard-sized. That way he can nurture every plant himself from start to finish—from selecting seeds for flavor versus hardiness, to planting crops to optimize sunlight and soil nourishment, to pruning each leaf and vine by hand and waiting until the produce reaches ripe perfection before bringing it to market. Every step in the process is guided by his artistic perfection.

Purpose provides an anchor point—not only in terms of specific goals or actions or how we choose to interpret our surprises, but also in terms of the overall impact that we want to have in the world. When there are trade-offs to be weighed, there are tough decisions to be made, or we're at a crossroads, we can use our clarity of purpose as a tie breaker, a fail-safe decision criterion that we know we can trust.

Questions to Consider

- ➲ When have you been at a crossroads and didn't know what do but then relied on your sense of purpose to show you the way? What happened?

- ➲ What is your deeper purpose beyond just selling something, offering something, or making money?

- ➲ What contribution do you want to make to others in the world?

➲ How can you make this contribution in ways that are both *smaller* and *larger* than you have imagined thus far?

"Telescoping" Keeps Us Agile and Adaptive

Humility isn't just important to help us tune into surprises. It's essential for dealing with our setbacks and recalibrating the scope of our ambitions to ensure that we find the balance between being bold and remaining realistic. In Chapter One, I shared the general definition of a business breakthrough. Naturally, depending on what we're striving for, the specific details of what we consider breakthroughs for ourselves and our organizations change. Yes, breakthroughs are breakthroughs only if they challenge assumptions and deliver greater value than what existed before. But their scope can vary. A breakthrough may not need to change the world per se, but simply change a neighborhood. It may not need to transform an industry, but simply transform a product. It may not need to reinvent a company, but simply reshape a department.

How we define business breakthroughs is up to each one of us and is influenced by our backgrounds, challenges, opportunities, values, hopes, and goals. The goal isn't to become locked into a particular definition of success. It's quite the opposite. "Telescoping" is what I call the process of continually adjusting our goals and approaches by dialing them back or scaling them up as we encounter constraints or find ways to expand our impact. Even in the face of setbacks that change the scale or scope of our breakthroughs, the objective is to continue to optimistically move things forward in whatever way we can. By holding onto our sense of purpose and using our humility to grease the skids, we start to see the full potential and limitations of our breakthroughs. We accelerate out of the failure zone and begin to seize our opportunities.

Questions to Consider

⊃ When have you rescoped a goal? What happened, and how did this affect your ability to keep things moving forward?

⊃ In what ways could you *reduce* the scope of your breakthrough without feeling that you're compromising your sense of purpose?

⊃ How could you *increase* the scope of your breakthrough to have an even bigger impact?

Making It Real

We explored examples that show how, when we look back from where we are at any given point in time, we can see how the various events and experiences of our lives add up to where we currently sit. We discussed how we can view our journeys as part of our destination, using humility to make us more amenable to experiencing surprise. We talked about "telescoping" and how we can scope up or scope back our goals and actions to get us closer and closer to our breakthroughs. And we looked at how our sense of purpose is always ready and available to be used as a guidepost to the future.

The goal of the last phase of the leapfrogging life cycle is to seize upon our circumstances. When we realize that everything we do and everything that happens are natural parts of our longer-term journey, we achieve the openness, agility, and flexibility that foster surprise and accelerate success.

 ## Leapfrogging Tools

1. Connect the Dots by Uncovering Your Stepping-Stones

We all have dots, but not all of us always connect them. Connecting the dots of your past helps you see the stepping-stones that you've taken to get to the present and that can also be used to shape your future. When you step back to do this, you can see that all of your circumstances are essentially stepping-stones—so you're able to appreciate and interpret them through a whole new lens. At first it may be easiest to look at major events as stepping-stones. With practice it starts to become possible to view both the bigger events and the seemingly insignificant occurrences or little surprises as clearly contributing to where you are today. Try the following exercise:

A. Brainstorm a list of events, milestones, and accomplishments that are the stepping-stones that got you to where you are today. Consider both big and small things.

B. When you connect the dots, what do you see? Did one thing lead to the next? What were the circumstances that allowed things to unfold in the way that they did? Are there themes or patterns at play?

C. Determine the implications for your breakthrough. In what ways can you tap into the patterns and themes of your stepping-stones to inform your path forward? How can you use your past to guide and accelerate your future?

By gaining awareness of your prior path, you can more easily see and interpret your new stepping-stones in real time as they arise. The next time you are surprised, ask yourself the meaning of the stone that you just turned over and how it might connect to the rest of the dots on your path.

2. Bust Your Ego

This one might be tough, but it's worth a shot. In order to open ourselves up to the power of surprise and remain flexible and adaptable on our journeys, we have to discover our blind spots and bust our egos. Start this process by completing the following template:

Ego Busters	Blind Spots
▪	▪
▪	▪
▪	▪
▪	▪
▪	▪
▪	▪
▪	▪

A. Create a bullet point list of your "Ego Busters"—times you were wrong, missed a big surprise or opportunity, made a big mistake, didn't know the answer, or anything else where you really stumbled or struggled. Try to list things that likely happened because of your preconceived ideas or a personal agenda that you held onto with too much rigidity.

B. List the "Blind Spots" that you believe were responsible for your ego busters. To come up with your blind spots,

consider what you see when you look at your entire list of
ego busters. How do these things make you feel (uneasy,
embarrassed, stressed-out, angry, etc.)? Why? What were
you assuming, doing, missing, or blind to that contributed
to each of your ego busters? What patterns do you see?
You might list things like "I assumed I always had the
right answer" or "Our team didn't listen to anyone else."

3. Find Humility

Great examples of humility are all around us. Create a list of
people you know who have the characteristic of humility. These
can be people in history (Martin Luther King Jr., Gandhi, Mother
Teresa, etc.) or—ideally—people whom you're acquainted with
personally or professionally. What have they done to demonstrate
humility? What are their personal characteristics? What *don't*
they do?

Reflecting on this list, as well as what you learned from the
activity on ego busting, review the core components of humility.
For each component, determine what types of things you can do
to overcome your blind spots and gain greater humility. What
can you start doing, stop doing, or continue doing?

Examples of People with Humility (Historical or People You Know)	Core Components of Humility	Things to Start, Stop, or Continue Doing to Gain Greater Humility
_____ _____	1. Be able to accurately assess abilities and achievements	
_____ _____	2. Acknowledge imperfections, knowledge gaps, and limitations	
_____ _____	3. Remain open to new ideas, conflicting information, and advice from others	
_____ _____	4. Keep accomplishments in perspective	
_____ _____	5. Appreciate the value of all things, including the various ways that people and things contribute to the world	

4. Telescope Your Goals

One way to sustain forward momentum is to "scope back" your goals when things get tough and "scope up" your goals when you find opportunities to expand your impact. Whether you reduce or expand the scope of your goals, they should always provide forward movement that connects to the core purpose of your breakthrough. Use the template below to list your current goals. Then use both sides to rewrite your goals in ways that both scope them back and scope them up. What do you see? What are the implications and opportunities?

"Scoped Back" Goal	Current Goals	"Scoped Up" Goal
	Goal #1:	
	Goal #2:	
	Goal #3:	
	Goal #4:	
	Goal #5:	
	Goal #6:	

You should revisit this type of telescoping activity on an ongoing basis as things evolve. Always list today's goals as you define them in the middle column first, and then go from there.

9

Bring It Home

I may not have gone where I intended to go, but I think I have ended up where I intended to be.

—Douglas Adams

In the town square of Tallinn, the capital of the Baltic country of Estonia, there's a hole-in-the-wall restaurant that's several hundred years old. When I walked by it, I couldn't help but be drawn in by the chalk-scrawled sign in front that read: *fair coffee and decent pies, soup full of elk*. I also noticed that every Western tourist who glanced up at this makeshift billboard smiled from ear to ear. How could you not? I'm convinced the three young Estonian women running this restaurant knew their audience well because their house was full. In around 300 BC, Aristotle said that "the secret to humor is surprise." Clearly it's also the secret to selling mediocre food. Actually, the coffee and pies were pretty good. I didn't order the soup full of elk.

A series of life changes combined with these types of light-hearted yet mind-jogging experiences helped me tune into the power of surprise as a unifying factor in challenging mindsets and creating breakthroughs. I described the main catalyst for this realization in the Introduction—a visit to a remarkable little café in Paris. But, as is usually the case when it comes to big shifts in one's point of view, there were other factors at play. Living in another country definitely helped broaden my perspective. It challenged my assumptions and constantly revealed new ways of doing business and living life. One night, for example, my wife and I got a crash course of sorts in the French medical system. We thought our younger daughter had broken her nose, which required a call to our French doctor. When he answered the phone—yes, the doctor answered his own phone!—he agreed to see her right away. At his office, he examined our daughter's nose and instructed us to take her for an X-ray at a lab down the street. We returned about an hour later, X-ray in hand. Fortunately, our daughter's nose was not broken—and neither was our bank account. The entire "retail" cost of two doctor visits plus X-rays totaled seventy-five U.S. dollars. And, as an extra bonus, our daughter got to take home her X-ray because, in France, patients are responsible for the care and keeping of their own medical records. Later, my wife and I half-joked that the cost of this type of accident could bankrupt an uninsured family in the United States.

Not every surprise was so refreshing, or inexpensive, though. Some of France's cultural quirks made us appreciate our former lives in San Francisco even more. French businesses, for example, generally don't get the whole "customer service" thing. I found this out the hard way when I had to call the electric company about our bill, and I realized that I had to pay for every minute I was on the line with them. I complained to a French friend about this and he told me to count my blessings. Call centers in France had actually improved recently—customers used to get charged for the hold time as well!

At various times and in various ways, everyone in my family struggled with adapting to life in France and the French culture. But through our year-long exploration, we experienced a variety of surprises that gave us all greater insight into our subtle and not-so-subtle assumptions about what's right, what's wrong, what's good, what's bad, what works well, and what doesn't. Whether we acknowledged it when it was happening or not, we were experiencing surprises every day, which led us all to modify our mindsets. Eight months into our adventure, our eleven-year-old daughter woke up one morning and said to us, "Mom, Dad, I'm not the same person I was when I came to Paris. I feel totally different now." My response was simple. "Me, too," I said.

I moved to Paris assuming that "getting away from it all" would allow me to concentrate on my writing. It did, but the real benefit was how the experience prepared me to see the power of surprise. While I was already in the thick of my writing, surprise had not entered my awareness as a core message of the book. Then I wandered through the aromatic smoke of roasting coffee beans and into Caféotheque. Of course, as I've said, I was delighted by the coffee and amazed by the radically different way its owners had structured the business. But, more important, I was inspired. I realized that I had experienced this kind of positive surprise many times during my own personal life and professional career. And that's when it all clicked. I was being surprised by how important surprise is! That realization was my turning point. In essence, the process of writing this book was mirroring its content.

I struggled to make sense of what felt like a divergence from my original plan, not to mention the fact that my publisher had approved my book under the guise of an entirely different focus. But deep down, I knew I could not ignore what I was seeing in my research and experiencing every day as an expat in Paris. My surprises helped me gain a fresh perspective on my personal life as well as on the past twenty years of my professional career. Disrupting my life in such a deliberate way provided me with a new lens through which I could more clearly see and understand dynamics that I had experienced as a business leader, consultant, and researcher. And while the shift was initially a big *unpleasant* surprise for my publisher, he eventually came around.

The Principles of Surprise

I'm a firm believer that the "tool du jour" will inevitably become the has-been business fad of tomorrow. When it really comes down to it, the most important part of this book isn't the leapfrogging life cycle, the LEAPS model, or the tools to use for leapfrogging. The most significant idea is that surprise pervades business and life. When we internalize this one fact alone, the power of surprise will remain with us as a co-conspirator throughout our personal and organizational journeys.

When I was a kid, I would start a book by skipping to the end and reading the very last sentence. I don't do that anymore. Instead, I just go to the beginning of the last chapter. Clearly, there's always room to work on one's own openness to surprise.

If you've just jumped to this last chapter too, I won't fight against your gut instincts. Here are the most important principles to remember about the power of surprise:

1. Surprises are everywhere and happening all the time.

2. Surprises are the most predictable things in business and in life.

3. Surprises challenge assumptions.

4. Surprises are guideposts to our futures.

5. Surprises can help us discover and shape ourselves and our organizations, since they reveal clues about our identity and direction.

6. When we tune into surprises, we experience them more often.

7. We create breakthroughs when we use surprise to shift our mindsets, challenge the status quo, and deliver unexpected solutions that positively surprise others.

While the goal of *Leapfrogging* is to foster breakthrough business success, it's hard to avoid acknowledging the personal nature of both the leapfrogging process and surprise itself. Shifting mindsets and attuning ourselves and our organizations to embrace uncertainty and savor surprise inherently require some level of transformation on the personal level—of ourselves and of others who join us on our journeys.

The Relativity of Surprise

Just about anytime I discuss surprise, the question comes up about whether there are different types of surprises. Most people naturally gravitate toward seeing surprises in two flavors: positive and negative. They're either good or bad. They help us or they hurt us. As I hope I've shown throughout this book, surprises are relative events. We can choose to experience them as opportunities, or we can let them pull us down. I want to clarify here that I'm specifically talking about surprises related to *business breakthroughs.*

While some might argue that all surprises in business and in life, no matter what they are, are ripe to be interpreted by the eye of the beholder, I think it's important to acknowledge the differences. Surprises in nonbusiness life can indeed involve personal catastrophes that are different from those generally occurring in our organizations—illnesses or the unexpected death of a loved one, for example. And it's a natural reaction to perceive these things as "bad."

When it comes to business breakthroughs, though, we have a choice in how we experience and use surprise. For some, viewing surprises as opportunities may come easy. For others, it may feel like an uphill battle. Whereas one person might naturally experience an unexpected setback as the chance to reframe their goals into something more realistic, another might view a similar event as a blow to self-esteem or a reason to abandon an idea altogether. When we start to view our surprises as containing messages and clues, the unexpected can become something that's experienced as neutral at worst and as an energizing, positive force at best.

The Paradox of Surprise

In his book *The Age of Paradox*, Charles Handy said, "We need a new way of thinking about our problems and our futures. My suggestion is the management of paradoxes, an idea which is itself a paradox, in that paradox can only be 'managed' in the sense of coping with [it]. . . . Paradoxes are like the weather, something to be lived with, not solved, the worst aspects mitigated, the best enjoyed and used as clues to the way forward. Paradox has to be *accepted*, coped with, and made sense of, in life, in work, in the community, and among nations."[69]

Harnessing surprise is a paradox. If we could truly "manage" surprise, then we would be removing the one element that makes surprise, well, surprising. It's an oxymoron to think we can manage something that's unpredictable by its very nature. And that's what makes harnessing surprise so powerful for those who learn how to embrace it.

Handy goes on to say: "Living with paradox is not comfortable or easy. It can be like walking in a dark wood on a moonless night. It is an eerie and, at times, a frightening experience. All sense of direction is lost; trees and bushes crowd in on you; wherever you step you bump into another obstacle; every noise and rustle is magnified; there is a whiff of danger; it seems safer to stand still than to move." When faced with a paradox, it's easy to let ourselves become paralyzed. There's no clear answer. Tension exists. Finding what feels like the right balance is usually required to unfreeze ourselves, our teams, and our organizations. But even when we do find a steady path, it may last only temporarily, since the scales will ultimately require readjusting to keep us moving forward.

Handy's description of paradoxes can easily be applied to the process of leapfrogging. Both leapfrogging and surprise are paradoxical in their own ways. Creating breakthroughs involves living with an inherent tension; it means using the journey through ambiguity and uncertainty as a source of clarity and innovation. Surprise, the true essence of uncertainty, enters the process by delivering direction when it's most needed. It's hard to get more paradoxical than that. If I've learned one thing from experiencing this paradox play out in my own life it's this: The secret to gaining control is letting go of the need for it.

The Cycle of Surprise

I have now returned from Paris and am back living in the San Francisco Bay Area. When we landed at the Washington, DC, airport on our return flight from France, the moment we walked into the terminal my older daughter turned to me and said, "People are so loud here!" My wife and I looked at each other and smiled. We had clearly returned home.

While my family has reassimilated into American society and culture, it's impossible to simply step back into the same lives we left here before moving to Europe. Our mindsets have changed. And, as a result, we have changed our behavior. No more jam-packed week-ends. No more rushed dinners. No more eating at the same restaurant twice in a row. Many more visits to the farmer's market. Taste-tests to find the best baguettes and coffee in the Bay Area. More weekend road trips to explore new neighborhoods and places that have always been in our backyard but we've been "too busy" to visit.

Writing this book delivered many surprises to me on both a personal and professional level. But perhaps the biggest one of all is that I now have an obsession for experiencing surprise. New mind-sets mandate change. And change reshapes mindsets. It's an endless feedback loop filled with breakthrough potential. And it's a journey well worth taking.

Notes

1. David Lebovitz, *The Sweet Life in Paris: Delicious Adventures in the World's Most Glorious—and Perplexing—City* (New York: Broadway Books, 2009).

2. Hilary Austen and Roger Martin, *Artistry Unleashed: A Guide to Pursuing Great Performance in Work and Life* (Toronto, Canada: University of Toronto Press, 2010).

3. http://money.cnn.com/magazines/fortune/fortune_archive/2005/12/12/8363128/index.htm

4. Gary Hamel and Bill Breen, *The Future of Management* (Boston, MA: Harvard Business School Press, 2007).

5. Jim Collins and Morten Hansen, *Great by Choice: Uncertainty, Chaos, and Luck—Why Some Thrive Despite Them All* (New York: HarperCollins Publishers, 2011).

6. http://www.referenceforbusiness.com/biography/F-L/FitzGerald-Niall-1945.html

7. http://www.dupontlegalmodel.com/provider-network/

8. http://www.cpaglobal.com/newlegalreview/4377/inside_dupont_legal_model

9. http://www.cpaglobal.com/newlegalreview/4377/inside_dupont_legal_model

10. http://www.cpradr.org/Resources/ALLCPRArticles/tabid/265/
    ID/77/The-Next-Level-Promoting-Diversity-in-the-ADR-Arena-
    MCC.aspx

11. http://www.usnews.com/education/blogs/on-education/2009/
    06/17/charter-schools-might-not-be-better

12. http://www.kipp.org/news/the-economist-work-hard-be-nice-

13. http://www.crainsnewyork.com/article/20110102/SUB/
    301029995

14. http://nymag.com/print/?/nymetro/news/culture/features/2996/

15. http://articles.nydailynews.com/2009-02-03/local/17916320_1_
    thrift-store-carroll-gardens-dresses

16. http://nymag.com/print/?/nymetro/news/culture/features/2996/

17. http://worldinquiry.case.edu/bankInnovationView.cfm?id
    Archive=364

18. http://www.ilj.org/publications/docs/Community_Wealth_
    Generation_for_Non_Profit_Sustainability.pdf

19. http://www.hnl.bcm.tmc.edu/cache/ABCNEWS_com%20%20
    Study%20The%20Brain%20Likes%20Surprises.htm

20. http://www.emory.edu/EMORY_REPORT/erarchive/2001/April/
    erApril.30/4_30_01berns.html

21. http://network.intuit.com/videos/854245583001/

22. http://www.phrma.org/media/releases/rrd-investment
    -us-biopharmaceutical-companies-reached-record-levels-2010

23. http://blogs.villagevoice.com/runninscared/2010/11/the_5_most_
    prof.php

24. http://www.oneworldhealth.org/diarrheal_disease

25. http://www.oneworldhealth.org/Letter_from_the_CEO

26. http://www.globalinnovationcommons.org/blog/victoria-hale
    -uncommon-hero-eradicating-black-fever-leishmaniasis

27. http://www.esquire.com/features/best-n-brightest-2005/
    ESQ1205B&BHALE_222

28. See Malcolm Gladwell, *The Tipping Point: How Little Things Can Make a Big Difference* (New York: Back Bay Books, 2002).

29. See W. Chan Kim and Renée Mauborgne, *Blue Ocean Strategy: How to Create Uncontested Market Space and Make Competition Irrelevant* (Boston, MA: Harvard Business School Publishing Corp., 2005).

30. See Clayton Christensen, *The Innovator's Dilemma: When New Technologies Cause Great Firms to Fall* (New York: Harper Paperbacks, 2003).

31. http://money.cnn.com/galleries/2008/fortune/0803/gallery .jobsqna.fortune/3.html

32. A. Dijksterhuis and L. F. Nordgren, "A Theory of Unconscious Thought," *Perspectives on Psychological Science* 1 (2006): 95–109.

33. http://money.cnn.com/galleries/2008/fortune/0803/gallery .jobsqna.fortune/3.html

34. http://www.loc.gov/law/find/hearings/pdf/00170203720.pdf

35. http://news.stanford.edu/news/2005/june15/jobs-061505.html

36. http://www.linktv.org/programs/nora!

37. William Maddux and Adam Galinsky, "Cultural Borders and Mental Barriers: The Relationship Between Living Abroad and Creativity," *Journal of Personality and Social Psychology* 96 (2009): 1047–1061.

38. Reprinted with permission from the American Psychological Association. William Maddux and Adam Galinsky. (2009). "Cultural Borders and Mental Barriers: The Relationship Between Living Abroad and Creativity," *Journal of Personality and Social Psychology* 96 (2009): 1047–1061. Published by the American Psychological Association.

39. http://www.newscenter.philips.com/main/standard/about/news/ press/article-15762.wpd

40. *The Wall Street Journal*, July 11, 2007, p. A1(2).

41. John Mullins and Randy Komisar, *Getting to Plan B: Breaking Through to a Better Business Model* (Boston, MA: Harvard Business School Publishing, 2009).

42. http://money.cnn.com/galleries/2008/fortune/0803/gallery.jobsqna.fortune/3.html

43. Peter Sims, *Little Bets: How Breakthrough Ideas Emerge from Small Discoveries* (New York: Free Press, 2011).

44. http://www.inc.com/magazine/20110201/how-great-entrepreneurs-think.html

45. http://www.google.com/jobs/lifeatgoogle/englife/index.html

46. http://www.economist.com/node/18557776

47. http://www.economist.com/node/18557776

48. http://www.geekwire.com/2011/amazons-bezos-innovation

49. http://www.fastcompany.com/magazine/78/jobs.html?page=0%2C1

50. http://news.stanford.edu/news/2005/june15/jobs-061505.html

51. Jennifer Lerner and Keltner Dacher, "Beyond Valence: Toward a Model of Emotion-Specific Influences on Judgment and Choice," *Cognition and Emotion* 14 (2000): 473–493.

52. http://www.geekwire.com/2011/amazons-bezos-innovation

53. Suzanne C. Segerstrom, Breaking Murphy's Law: *How Optimists Get What They Want from Life and Pessimists Can Too* (New York: Guilford Press, 2006).

54. Research study conducted by Lise Solberg Nes, a graduate student of Segerstrom.

55. Jill Neimark, "The Optimism Revolution," *Psychology Today*, May/June 2007, pp. 88–94.

56. Ibid.

57. D. R. Carney, A. J. C. Cuddy, and A. J. Yap, "Power Posing: Brief Nonverbal Displays Affect Neuroendocrine Levels and Risk Tolerance," *Psychological Science* 21 (2010): 1–6.

58. Ibid. Copyright © 2010 by Sage Publications. Reprinted by Permission of SAGE Publications.

59. http://www.wfu.edu/wfunews/2003/021903f.html

60. http://www.cnn.com/2011/10/05/us/obit-steve-jobs/

61. http://www.wmagazine.com/w/blogs/editorsblog/2009/11/24/five -minutes-with-frances-haut.html

62. B. Nevicka et al., "Reality at Odds with Perceptions: Narcissistic Leaders and Group Performance," *Psychological Science* 22 (2011): 1259–1264.

63. http://www.inc.com/articles/201106/the-humility-imperative -ceos-keep-your-arrogance-in-check.html

64. J. P. Tangney, "Humility: Theoretical Perspectives, Empirical Findings and Directions for Future Research," *Journal of Social and Clinical Psychology* 19 (2000): 70–82.

65. http://online.wsj.com/article/SB1000142405270230437030457515 2133860888958.html

66. http://www.etsy.com/teams/7718/site-help/discuss/6796377/ page/1/

67. http://www.inc.com/magazine/20110401/can-rob-kalin-scale-etsy .html?nav=fly

68. http://online.wsj.com/article/SB1000142405270230437030457515 2133860888958.html

69. Charles Handy, *The Age of Paradox* (Boston, MA: Harvard Business School Press, 1995).

Acknowledgments

Although I'm the named author, this book reflects the experiences, insights, and ideas of many people:

My mentors and coaches: Neil Maillet and Jesse Powell, who, each in his own way, pushed me outside of my comfort zone and helped me learn how my "voice"—my knowledge, experiences, and qualities as a person—can be heard through my writing;

My colleagues and partners: Sally Crawford, Jeannette de Noord, Bob Krinsky, James McCoy, Diane Nijs, Derrick Palmer, Barbara Talbott, and Stu Winby, who continually challenge my thinking and collaborate with me to trail-blaze new paths that would otherwise remain uncharted;

My friends and clients: Massimo d'Amore, Gloria Montenegro de Chirouze, Bernard Chirouze, Tina Christopoulou, Tena Clark, Cassie Divine, Mehmood Khan, Ellen Marram, Sarah Robb O'Hagan, Steve Paljieg, Allyson Phillips, Chuck Templeton, and Robyn Waters, who contributed candid comments and compelling stories about their breakthroughs to help convey the often unspoken leadership and organizational success factors involved in bringing big ideas to life;

My family: Holli, my wife, who served as sounding board, thinking partner, reality-checker, editor, and personal motivator during the year-long journey of writing this book; Raelyn, my older daughter, who everyday models how to think and act like a true leapfrogger; Nola, my younger daughter, whose fearlessness and rock-solid sense of self are ever-present inspirations; and the rest of my family, who have given their unconditional support, encouragement, and love, both in life and around this book.

And to all those who took but a small risk and have elected to read *Leapfrogging*—thank you for joining me on this journey. I hope you gleaned a surprise or two reading it. I know I did writing it.

Index

About the Author

Soren Kaplan is a California native whose grandparents immigrated to the United States from France. His dual American–French citizenship, combined with a family heritage rooted in art, design, education, and religion instilled in him an appreciation for diverse experiences, cultures and a life chock full of surprise. Soren has worked within large corporations, has founded and advises start–ups, consults to global companies, and educates students and executives about the art and discipline of strategic thinking, innovation and leadership for business breakthroughs. His unique ability to uncover surprises that are "hidden in plain sight" helps leaders shift their mindsets to rethink and reinvent their organizations.

As a co–founder and managing principal of InnovationPoint, Soren leads strategic initiatives and provides leadership development for organizations including Colgate–Palmolive, Disney, Kimberly–Clark, PepsiCo, Visa, Aviva (United Kingdom), Grundfos (Denmark), Philips (The Netherlands), SK Telecom (South Korea), Tekes (Finland), and numerous other firms. He has conducted workshops in Shanghai, managed meetings in Topeka, and he was once stranded in Helsinki thanks to the Icelandic volcano.

Soren is also an Adjunct Professor within the Imagineering Academy at NHTV Breda University of Applied Sciences in The Netherlands. He previously led the Business Innovation & Technology Solutions group at Hewlett–Packard (HP) during the roaring 1990s in the Silicon Valley, and then co–founded iCohere, one of the first web collaboration software platforms for online learning and communities of practice. He holds Master's and Ph.D. degrees in Organizational Psychology and resides in the San Francisco Bay Area with his wife, two daughters, and hypo–allergenic cat.

For more information visit www.leapfrogging.com. You can contact Soren from the "contact" link at the website.

Berrett–Koehler
Publishers

Berrett-Koehler is an independent publisher dedicated to an ambitious mission: *Creating a World That Works for All*.

We believe that to truly create a better world, action is needed at all levels—individual, organizational, and societal. At the individual level, our publications help people align their lives with their values and with their aspirations for a better world. At the organizational level, our publications promote progressive leadership and management practices, socially responsible approaches to business, and humane and effective organizations. At the societal level, our publications advance social and economic justice, shared prosperity, sustainability, and new solutions to national and global issues.

A major theme of our publications is "Opening Up New Space." Berrett-Koehler titles challenge conventional thinking, introduce new ideas, and foster positive change. Their common quest is changing the underlying beliefs, mindsets, institutions, and structures that keep generating the same cycles of problems, no matter who our leaders are or what improvement programs we adopt.

We strive to practice what we preach—to operate our publishing company in line with the ideas in our books. At the core of our approach is stewardship, which we define as a deep sense of responsibility to administer the company for the benefit of all of our "stakeholder" groups: authors, customers, employees, investors, service providers, and the communities and environment around us.

We are grateful to the thousands of readers, authors, and other friends of the company who consider themselves to be part of the "BK Community." We hope that you, too, will join us in our mission.

A BK Business Book

This book is part of our BK Business series. BK Business titles pioneer new and progressive leadership and management practices in all types of public, private, and nonprofit organizations. They promote socially responsible approaches to business, innovative organizational change methods, and more humane and effective organizations.

Berrett–Koehler
Publishers

A community dedicated to creating
a world that works for all

Visit Our Website: www.bkconnection.com

Read book excerpts, see author videos and Internet movies, read our authors' blogs, join discussion groups, download book apps, find out about the BK Affiliate Network, browse subject-area libraries of books, get special discounts, and more!

Subscribe to Our Free E-Newsletter, the *BK Communiqué*

Be the first to hear about new publications, special discount offers, exclusive articles, news about bestsellers, and more! Get on the list for our free e-newsletter by going to **www.bkconnection.com**.

Get Quantity Discounts

Berrett-Koehler books are available at quantity discounts for orders of ten or more copies. Please call us toll-free at (800) 929-2929 or email us at bkp .orders@aidcvt.com.

Join the BK Community

BKcommunity.com is a virtual meeting place where people from around the world can engage with kindred spirits to create a world that works for all. BKcommunity.com members may create their own profiles, blog, start and participate in forums and discussion groups, post photos and videos, answer surveys, announce and register for upcoming events, and chat with others online in real time. Please join the conversation!

MIX
Paper from
responsible sources
FSC® C012752
www.fsc.org

Certified

Corporation
bcorporation.net